"This is recommended reading for our 3200 representatives, who are among the finest trained professionals in America today."
  –Michael A. White
  President and CEO
  American Counselors, Inc.

"Much of life is a sales process, and I can think of no better primer for it than Smart Salespeople Sometimes Wear Plaid.*"*
  –Stephen L. Enoch
  Business Manager
  Lewis Grizzard Enterprise, Inc.

"A brilliant combination of sound information and winning advice, stimulating, witty, and enjoyable."
  –Pinckney "Kip" Ridley
  Senior National Sales Director
  Primerica Financial Services

"In reality you can only invest two things — your time and your money. This is one sales and business book worthy of both."
  –Randall J. Yeoman
  Senior Principal, Cofounding Principal
  Investors Group First Plan

SMART SALESPEOPLE
SOMETIMES
WEAR PLAID

Dare to Be Extraordinary
in a Mediocre World

Barry Graham Munro

Prima Publishing
P.O. Box 1260BK
Rocklin, CA 95677
(916) 632-4400

Production by Bookman Productions
Copyediting by Elizabeth von Radics
Typography by Page Design, Inc.
Interior design by Bookman Productions
Cover design by The Dunlavey Studio, Sacramento

Library of Congress Cataloging-in-Publication Data
Munro, Barry Graham.
Smart salespeople sometimes wear plaid: dare to be extraordinary in a mediocre world/Barry Graham Munro.
p. cm.
Includes index.
ISBN 1-55958-422-X (pbk.)
1. Selling. I. Title.
HF5438.25.M85 1994
658.85 —dc20   93-34369
CIP

95 96 97 98 RRD 10 9 8 7 6 5 4 3 2
Printed in the United States of America

How to Order:
Single copies may be ordered from Prima Publishing, P.O. Box 1260BK, Rocklin, CA 95677; telephone (916) 632-4400. Quantity discounts are also available. On your letterhead, include information concerning the intended use of the books and number of books you wish to purchase.

CONTENTS

ACKNOWLEDGMENTS

I would like to thank my wife Sheila and daughters, Tosha and Tara, for their love, support and inspiration, and to all my special friends for their allegiance and understanding then and now. Thank you, Lord, for such undeserved blessings.

A special thanks to: Joan L. Day; my great friend David Landrum; Charla Necaise; David A. Vigilanti, the stepfather who was a father; and Carol Munro, the great encourager.

ABOUT THE AUTHOR

Barry Graham Munro makes his home in Atlanta, Georgia, with his wife, two daughters, and six hundred pounds of sporting equipment. Born in Canada, he grew up with a zeal for history and competitive sports which translates into all of his writing. Turning from a desire to teach, he began a sales career in advertising. Here he excelled in selling and servicing regional, then national accounts in print media. From this, he joined the rapidly growing financial service industry where he quickly moved into management and brokered various financial products. Here he found a niche, and specialized in training, motivating, and building sales and marketing teams. An independent thinker, Barry has the unique ability to synthesize information and then relate it to others in a meaningful yet entertaining way. As a highly sought-after speaker and media guest, Barry loves people and his work. His goal is to produce books and training programs that portray fun and realistic approaches to winning in sales, management, and leadership. Barry's mother says he's a good boy who always calls home!

Look for his upcoming book *The Plaid Manager.*

INTRODUCTION

Consider the plaid pattern. Its enduring
strength lies in its design, which is colorful
yet always under control.

If you could wish for anything in the world, what would you wish for? Would it be fame? Fortune? Would it be love or power? And what about youth? Sooner or later that's a good one. Anyway, while you're thinking, let me relate to you a short story and the reason for this book.

I suppose it started in earnest the day I landed my first real job after college. I say *real* job because the first two couldn't possibly qualify. One of these was working at a gas station, where I learned the useful art of communicating through Plexiglas. The other was distributing coupons for a local businessman. This guy was the P. T. Barnum of the South; he believed there was a sucker born every minute, and it was my time to be it. These first two jobs were a somber initiation into the real world of red ink versus black ink, and Easy Street versus the salt mines of the eternally doomed. So you can imagine my excitement when I found that a large daily newspaper actually believed my résumé and was hiring me for its advertising department. Why, they paid a salary plus bonus, all my insurance, and I got a week of vacation after twelve months of service! Finally, **I had the chance to make my mark!**

Oh, did I happen to mention this job was in sales? That's right, sales. But what did I know about selling? Not much, I'm afraid, although I did have some contact with the selling world; my father was always in sales and he was darn good. So, I guess growing up I was surrounded by it. In fact, now that I think of it, I remember my mother telling the story of how at five years old I sold a roll of expired raffle tickets to all our neighbors. I then proudly came home with a pocketful of cash, which to my amazement and horror my mother quickly made me return. This was a classic case in selling of Mother's Remorse.

Anyway, I was going into sales like my father. I thought about that for a while, reminiscing, and then something unsettling came to my attention. Years earlier I remember my father telling me that selling was a great way of life, but you've got to be careful because salespeople are sometimes used and abused. At the time, of course, I dismissed this rather harsh assessment. After all, you know how fathers can be. Maybe it was tax time and he was stressed out, or possibly he was experiencing that male menopause thing and couldn't afford a sports car. Who knows? After a few years of experience in sales, however, I couldn't ignore it anymore! As usual, I found that my father was right, he just wasn't born to the diplomatic corps. This concurrence of opinion with my father has come from observing a number of talented salespeople, many of whom started their careers so promisingly yet ended up burned out, broken, or thoroughly disillusioned. **It seems only a select few would find the secrets needed to win the selling game.** How's that for an oil spill in the crystal blue sea of happy endings?

But who's to blame for these sad endings to some careers? There's got to be a scapegoat out there somewhere, doesn't there? Well, not really. In fact, I don't blame anyone. I believe that's simply the way things are sometimes and if you don't know how things are, then caveat emptor; or should I say, *seller* beware? True, there are a few employers who take advantage of salespeople, but this is a small minority overall. I found that most of the problems encountered by salespeople are caused by their own ignorance of selling, which in turn causes them to make predictable mistakes over and over again.

Take myself for instance: Was I green when I started! It seems most of us start out this way because we never planned to go into sales in the first place. It just sort of happened, and letting things happen to you instead of making things happen for you can be a dangerous practice. Rough estimates figure only 5 percent of business graduates express a desire to go into sales. Yet after only ten years in the workplace up to 75 percent of this same group are involved in, you guessed it, sales.

At present, with economies becoming more service oriented and less manufacturing related, the demand for salespeople seems to be steadily rising. Add to this the tremendous glut of marketing majors who fill our colleges and universities and we are assured the sales arena will continue to have a good supply of green recruits in the future. Like myself, these young hopefuls will stumble into the selling world having no idea of how it works or how to work it. Whimsically most envision themselves putting in a few good years and then moving effortlessly up the management ladder. Why not? That's what happens to people in accounting, isn't it? Maybe, but don't count on such predictability when it comes to sales. It's a more complex world; that's why it pays so well.

Crash Course

Of course, once I saw that my future was in sales I decided to do some in-depth research to learn as much as possible about this strange subject. Like most, this prompted me to purchase my first book on selling. Admittedly, I was none too comforted after reading chapter one, which began by telling me I shouldn't be ashamed of being in sales. Why? Because sales was no longer a job, it was now a profession. Boy, that helped!

Reading further, I was slowly put at ease with many reassuring tips. Sales would be easy, according to this book; all I had to do was wear a dark blue suit with a red tie, follow a 146-point selling technique, and use its patented power phrases. It seemed this system was infallible because it was based on an ancient grid handed down by the Druids and formulated when Mars was on the cusp of Saturn, or was it Pluto? Well, the book wasn't *that* bad, but I wish I had possessed this book in its place. **I wanted to win and I know this book would have been an immense help.** Why? Because this book is not formulated by academics who have never sold, but is based on proven methods used by the best salespeople of today. It's not just a pump-up manual, yet it is motivating. In other words, it has a practical mix of the fundamentals and the intangibles.

In general, salespeople fall into one of three stages of development: the **natural,** the **self-made,** and the **master.** The naturals have great ability, but because this ability comes so easily they seldom perfect their gift. The second type, the self-made, have to work harder to compensate for their lack of talent, but this hard work eventually raises their performance level to that of the naturals. Satisfied, this is where they stay. Then there is the master. The masters hail from both groups, but they have chosen to perfect their selling skills to the highest level through education, practice, memorization, experience, and attention to detail. **The master knows what to say and do in all situations.** The master is prepared, and that's what this book is all about. Safe to say, if you want to reach top levels of income and achievement, you must become a master salesperson. The master is the extraordinary individual rising above the mediocre!

Well, since those early days I have read many books on selling, and most have proven to be of value. I've had the opportunity to learn firsthand from some of the best managers and salespeople in the business. This plus experience and time helped me acquire the basic skills. These fundamentals, with hard work and trial and error, helped me consistently earn an income at the top of my field. Still, the wish remained for a book that could totally encapsulate everything one would need to know to be successful in sales. With this thought in mind, I set about to compose a special book which would do just that. And thus was born *Smart Salespeople Sometimes Wear Plaid.*

In this complete business trainer we explore the A to Z of selling. From appointment making and handling objections to closing sales and getting referrals, we reveal the latest thinking and the advanced mechanics of sales with tips and techniques to improve selling skills no matter what level you're at. Along with these fundamentals is a wealth of information which is perhaps even more important to your overall success in selling. **It's critical to realize that just gaining knowledge of the mechanics of sales will not guarantee long-term success.** From experience I've come to see that almost anybody can learn to sell if they're taught how. Sadly, though, only a few will go on to master the art of winning in their sales careers. This, then, provides the missing link to their ultimate success.

So besides greatly enhancing your selling skills, this book also shares information to help ensure a winning sales career, like how to survive and prosper in sales by making and keeping more money; how to handle the real competition; how to win with bonus plans; how to promote yourself and get along with people; the importance of service; and whether you should go into management; plus, how to make good decisions regarding job and career changes. This and much more are the things the extraordinary salesperson knows, and they are of immeasurable value in advancing a sales career.

In relation to this point, I have found, with very few exceptions, that the big producers in business constantly update their knowledge by reading and studying; on the other hand, the mediocre seldom take this practice to heart. Perhaps this is because, like most, they tend to overestimate their current abilities and see themselves as above average. Too bad their numbers don't show it. Of course, some say they listen to tapes instead. Well, I use tapes too, but it's my contention that nothing affords the indelible transfer of knowledge better than reading. Listening to tapes is acceptable, but it can be quite passive and your concentration can wander, especially in a car. On the other hand, reading is active and demands exclusive concentration. When you read, the speed and emphasis is controlled by you, plus you are able to take notes as well as highlight.

A recent study done on successful people determined that more than any other factor earning power is governed primarily by mastery of word skill, which is naturally developed by reading. No doubt the famous British actor, Michael Caine, knew this firsthand. When Caine was once asked why he thought, as a poor cockney child from the wrong side of the tracks, that he could make it, he said he got the idea from books. **"From books I knew that all things were possible."**

Today a reader, tomorrow a leader. So, to make sure this book affords you a good success rate when read, it's purposely presented in a comfortable typeface and an entertaining format, paying tribute to the idea that the real sign of a master teacher is simplicity.

You'll find that *Smart Salespeople Sometimes Wear Plaid* is filled with humor, great stories, and usable quotes and anecdotes. This is to ensure that it will be valued and read, not just by the sales scholars but by all those who earn their keep by persuasion. For ease of reference, the book has been divided into three parts with a total of sixteen chapters. Part 1 deals with the main themes attached to winning. Part 2 is a complete nuts-and-bolts look at the fundamentals of big-time selling. Part 3 acts as an adviser on career management decisions. Each section is an integral part of the whole concept. It's important to note that great value will be derived from reading any one of these sections; however, the greatest benefit will go to those who persevere and complete all three. I especially feel you'll find Part 3 worth the wait. Also, you should know, that **many managers have found it helpful to have their**

people read just one chapter per week. This chapter can then be discussed during a portion of the weekly meeting. This is an easy goal to accomplish and works out nicely, since each chapter represents a different subject. Safe to say, these managers have a training tool people will really use.

Now, do you remember when I asked you what you would wish for? Well, ages ago another person was asked this same question. After only a short deliberation, this man, Solomon, wished for something special. He wished for what few people would consider. He wished for wisdom. In asking for wisdom, Solomon acquired the golden key to obtaining all good things: wealth, power, health, happiness, and the admiration of his contemporaries. It's a wonderful old story; however, time has not changed a thing. Today the acquisition of wisdom is just as profitable as it was in Solomon's time.

Which brings me to the purpose for this book: The most valuable tool to have in one's possession in sales is also wisdom. However, **wisdom is not just knowledge, but the sound application of that knowledge.** It is my humble yet passionate belief that by reading, studying, and rereading *Smart Salespeople Sometimes Wear Plaid,* you will find much of the wisdom needed to work, manage, and win big in your sales career.

About the Title

Is there any meaning behind the peculiar title to this book? Yes. You may have noticed that my last name is Munro, and as a history major I was always intrigued by the origin of this Scottish name. One day, by chance, I had the opportunity to talk to a true Scotsman who shared my enthusiasm for the past. I asked him about my name, and from a book he showed me the plaid pattern he called a tartan, which identified a member of the Munro clan. Then he said something I'll never forget. He said, **"Consider the plaid tartan, laddie; its enduring strength lies in its design, which is colorful yet always under control."** You know, when you stop to think about it, those are the main qualities to possess in any endeavor, especially sales.

Why? Perhaps the definition of the words *color* and *control* as applied to ourselves will help to explain. *Color* is defined as the quality that distinguishes otherwise indistinguishable objects from one another. Equating this to people, color is our individuality, talent, and imagination. Color is what makes us different from everyone else. The word *control,* on the other hand, is noted as the ability to regulate and command. In human terms, control is one's capacity to discipline oneself. So color is our individual talent, and control is our discipline factor. With this established, if you closely examine any successful person, you will find both these qualities existing in balance. I think this saying will bring this idea into focus (excuse the gender references).

> If you have Talent (color) and Discipline (control)
> You can become King.
> If you have little Talent but possess good Discipline,
> You can still become Prince.
> However, if you have tremendous Talent but possess
>   no Discipline,
> You risk becoming a Pauper.

This paradox of color versus control is an underexplored area of self-development. To address this need, I have devised a Color Versus Control Personality Test, which I give in speaking and seminar work. For your benefit I have included this popular test in the appendix of this book. It can be used as a management and self-evaluation tool, giving you a general idea of your talent-to-discipline ratio. Albeit entertaining and practical, it also gives people an idea of what their strengths and weaknesses are. At any rate, I owe the whole idea to the old Scotsman who pointed out the perfect balance of color and control within the tartan design. So with this story and the meaning behind it, I say, "Smart salespeople sometimes wear plaid." Of course, in recommending the merits of plaid, I also suggest moderation and good taste. No kilts or loud double knits, please!

THE FOUNDATIONS
OF WINNING

An acre of performance is worth a world of promise.
W.D. HOWELLS

Fortune favors the brave.
JOHN NEWCOMBE

1

ATTITUDE:
THE ULTIMATE
SELF-PROPHECY

Success is never final and failure never fatal.
It's courage that counts.
GEORGE F. TILTON

Show me a hardworking person with little in their possession but a great attitude, and I'll show you someone headed for success. On the other hand, present me with a person who has developed a poor attitude, and I'll show you a person destined to climb no higher. Needless to say, the importance of having and maintaining a positive attitude cannot be underestimated or trivialized.

Attitude has firmly entrenched itself as one of those great buzzwords often overheard in the business world. Unfortunately, the big problem with buzzwords is that sooner or later they lose their buzz. I suppose this is because with increased use we gradually become desensitized to them. Take the word *inflation*. We've heard this one so often we're basically apathetic to it. It's only when we attempt to buy a new home or car that we realize the ravages and true meaning of inflation. Words can definitely lose their impact, but this doesn't change their reality one bit.

I count myself as fortunate to live in a golf community, inhabited by some very successful salespeople and sales managers. Because the city we live in is a major hub for the southeastern United States, these successful people represent most of the large national and international companies, everything from AT&T and IBM to Coca Cola and Kimberly Clark, or, as I say, "everything from telephones to tissue paper." These people are a savvy group, but surprisingly modest and open. I presume they're a lot like you. Anyway, while walking the course, I like to quiz these people and listen to their ideas on sales and management. It's not surprising to find a variety of opinions on various topics from empowerment to Bonus plans; when I ask these executives what's the most important factor in determining a salesperson's or sales manager's long-term success, however, the answer is always the same: **Attitude, Attitude, Attitude!** Funny, I would have thought someone would answer hard work, or product knowledge, or even my answer, marrying the owner's son or daughter. But they consistently place attitude at the very top of the list. That's because: **Attitude controls behavior.**

First of all, just what is a good attitude and where do we get one? Some folks think having a good attitude means walking around saying fun things like, "Gee, I feel great" or "Hey, I'm a winner" or the ever popular "Business is booming." These statements are certainly signs of a good attitude, but they are only surface indicators. After all, most people in sales and management today know all the right things to say. The question is, do they really believe them? In reality a great attitude is a by-product of belief, and *belief* is just another word for faith. So a good attitude does not stem from what you say or how you feel. It has its real basis in what you have *chosen to believe*. Let's look at the facts.

ATTITUDE

FACT ONE: *Mental position is a matter of choice.*

Let's get it straight from the start. In the big leagues, all of us are faced with numerous difficulties and challenges. That's part of the deal. And you can't always control the stimuli life will present you. Still, never forget that you can control the response you give to these stimuli by choosing to react either positively or negatively. A positive · response would be one where you hold to the belief that any difficulty encountered is only temporary and just a necessary part of reaching your final objective. You would have faith and believe in your eventual triumph and the attainment of your goal.

A negative response, on the other hand, would illicit not faith, but fear. This is where you would be expressing doubt that you could reach your goal. The way you choose to respond is totally up to you. In truth, attitude is the only thing on this planet that you determine 100 percent of the time, so ultimately, you decide the outlook that you live with regardless of circumstances. What attitude have you chosen? Have you made the right choice?

FACT TWO: *Nothing good in life can be accomplished without a positive belief in its achievement.*

Think of it this way. The symbol for positive is the + sign, which is also the symbol for addition. In business, to achieve something greater than your current status you must add something to it—possibly more effort, or more belief. The plus or positive symbol represents this addition. Likewise, in order not to achieve or to achieve less than your current status, you must subtract, which is the negative or minus sign (−). This subtraction could be represented by less effort, less belief, or less persistence in achieving your goal. Some people may point out the importance of expressing both the positive and the negative in your life, kind of like the Chinese cosmological view of existence, the yin and yang. Admittedly, I don't understand all the relationships of the positive to the negative and of the Chinese yin and yang, although I have been up to my yingyang in trouble before. I do know, however, that negative destroys and positive builds. Therefore, logically, the smart salesperson or sales manager who is a builder will strive to be positive at all times.

FACT THREE: *You can achieve a positive attitude only when you believe good things will happen to you.*

Alabama football's coach Bear Bryant used to say "There are winners who know they are winners, losers who have decided they can never win, and finally there are the folks who haven't won yet but think they can." What factor helps form these different attitudes? Primarily it is the degree to which a person believes they deserve success.

The deep-rooted belief that good things should happen to you is the foundation on which all good attitudes are built. I have met a number of people who were considered by others as afraid to succeed; after closer examination, however, I've found that the real problem wasn't a fear of success so much as a belief that they didn't deserve success.

It seems that many people carry a burden of guilt and inferiority, which has convinced them they're not worthy to succeed. Perhaps such feelings of low self-esteem stem from an underprivileged background, or illiteracy, or maybe abuse. Whatever the reason, left unchecked, such an outlook inevitably hinders their upward climb in the business world.

Of course, all of us at times doubt our abilities to succeed. But believing we have no *right* to win is a much more serious matter. Such people, for instance, will continuously put themselves down and demean their own actions. They will say things like, "Gee, just my luck, things never work out for me" or "If I tried that, I would really mess it up" or the ever-popular "I could never do that." Sadly, you'll also find these people extra-eager to blame themselves for everything, unlike the more common reaction of trying to pass the buck.

Another big tip-off to self-image problems may be observed when these people are on the verge of success. A shutdown mechanism seems to automatically kick in and override their behavior; suddenly, they may stop working as hard, or they may become sick, or even quit outright, ultimately sabotaging any chance for success. Such a pattern in a salesperson's career almost invariably indicates a poor self-image. This is vital because your self-image determines exactly where you'll end up.

To be truly successful, you have to hold firm to the belief that you deserve to achieve. It's your right! Thus guilt, blame, and self-deprecation must be dealt with before you can truly achieve a positive attitude that allows you to win. The extraordinary salespeople have first made peace with themselves and their past, and fully believe they deserve success as much as the next person.

FACT FOUR: *Nothing affects your attitude more than the environment in which you choose to operate.*

I vividly recall as a youngster watching my father try to fix various things around the house. He would start in fine shape but inevitably his experiments in carpentry, plumbing, and electronics would end in disaster. Once frustrated, he would utter a few choice words and then call a professional to fix the problem and the greater fiasco he created. With this background, it's not hard to guess what my approach is when tackling domestic chores. My father couldn't program me to be a Mr. Fix-it, but to his credit he gave me great training in the use of colorful language. It was only when I went to work for a builder one summer during college that I learned, by example, how to successfully negotiate the puzzling world of home repairs. The point of all this is, like it or not, you are a product of your environment and a tiger can't change its stripes.

In relationship to this point, there's a great metaphysical debate going on which has recently intensified. In simplistic terms, one school strongly believes that we should seek all the answers we need from within ourselves, that the answers are there if we just discover how to tap into them. In other words, each of us is totally complete within ourself. The other school in this debate believes that no one is self-sufficient and each person needs constant outside input.

I side with the latter opinion because it's my belief that **you can never create anything greater than yourself by yourself.** This is especially true in regard to attitude. Here you really must have input, for just like a computer that can accomplish only what it has been programmed to, we, as humans, cannot function in a vacuum, oblivious to outside influences. In relationship to attitude, we must have positive input to produce positive output; or in plain, down-home language, you are who you hang around with, and what you read and watch. As the old Latin proverb painfully points out, If you always live with those who are lame, you yourself will start to limp. So it's vital to always be aware of the positive and negative impact of your surroundings.

Naturally, if you desire a positive attitude, you'll have to shun the "doom and gloom" crowd and seek to associate with achievers who will inspire and guide you by their positive example. These people will act as mentors, helping you expand your vision. You must also be very careful to use books and other media to your attitude's advantage. Don't underestimate these powerful inputs; they can have a tremendous impact.

As we know, leaders are readers. Leaders by nature are constantly recharging others with positive input, which helps them, in turn, to achieve their own goals. But who recharges the recharger? Truly every leader needs to have a power source, and with all the literature available today there is no excuse not to tap into positive and inspirational material. Personally, I read biographies, stories of men and women who have accomplished great things throughout history. Their examples of achievement help to inspire and recharge my belief in times of self-doubt and discouragement. The object is to surround yourself with positive models in your reading, viewing, and associations, because you will eventually become like the people and things that influence you.

FACT FIVE: *Feelings should not dictate attitude.*

The most successful people in sales and management share a unique characteristic: They have the uncommon ability to show a consistently positive attitude. On the other hand, the not-so-successful have attitudes that fluctuate like a barometer in July. For these people, the only determining factor in forming their attitude is how they feel. If they are happy, they correspondingly form a positive attitude. The problem with this philosophy is that happiness for the most part depends on sheer happenstance. For instance, I have a new car, therefore I'm happy. I just closed a big sale, I'm happy. I received a promotion, I'm really happy; and now that I'm so happy, I can be positive to everyone. But, what happens when the circumstances change? What happens when the new car loses its luster? What happens if you don't receive that promotion? Are you still positive?

For many, when confronted with such negative occurrences, the first casualty is their positive attitude. However, a real positive attitude is never held captive to feelings and circumstances, whether good or bad. A true positive attitude will rise above the daily fluctuations and portray a confidence in long-term victory. This may seem obvious in its explanation, but it's almost oblivious to detection when practiced. The reason is that when a person portrays a true positive attitude on a consistent basis, other people often think it's because that person doesn't have any problems. Nothing could be farther from the truth. The real reason behind this positive outlook is that this person has made a conscious choice to be positive in spite of contrary feelings. It's not an act, but a necessary step toward winning.

To accomplish anything good in life, you must pass through at least three stages: the **dreaming stage,** the **doing stage,** and the **delivery** or **reward stage.** The winner has learned that to successfully negotiate all three stages he or she must consistently apply the pressure of an enthusiastic spirit. Against this no obstacle can stand. In truth, the real power to win comes from staying as excited and energetic in the doing stage as you were in the dreaming stage. After the dreaming stage, this is the hardest work you'll ever do!

My Favorite Attitude

Truly the most enduring symbol of the British spirit is Winston Churchill, a statesman, soldier, artist, and, fortunately for our benefit, a brilliant author. He has left volumes of great work. From his award-winning six-part masterpiece, *The Second World War,* come four simple lines that to me epitomize the perfect attitude:

> In War, Resolution
> In Defeat, Defiance
> In Victory, Magnanimity
> In Peace, Goodwill

The first line, "In War, Resolution," refers to a mortal struggle between opposing forces, but an analogy can be made to any endeavor in which we encounter resistance. For to be resolute is to display an attitude of commitment and positive confidence in ultimate victory.

The only real losers in life are those who never try and those who stop fighting. The second line of Churchill's alludes to the importance of consistency of attitude: We are never to give up no matter what the odds; we must always fight until our task is completed. A despairing attitude is defeatist and bankrupt of hope; but in defiance, hope is kept alive until victory replaces it. Besides giving some of the most lengthy, intricately crafted speeches ever heard, Churchill also has the distinction of giving one of the shortest talks on record. It happened when he was the highly publicized speaker for an American college graduating class of 1953. Everyone anticipated an evening of brilliant oratory from this larger-than-life figure, but when Churchill approached the microphone he said only this: **"Never give up, never give up, never, never, never."** He then sat back down. Despite the brevity of this address, no one felt they had been shortchanged. Churchill had said it all!

For the third line to be of any use to me, I first had to know what *magnanimity* meant. When I looked it up, it read, "to be forgiving and high minded." To illustrate this idea I can think of no better story than an episode from the life of Gen. Robert E. Lee. It seems President Jefferson Davis once asked for Lee's evaluation of a certain officer in his command. Without hesitation, Lee gave a glowing recommendation of this officer's ability. All of this was overheard by a close friend of Lee's, who quickly took the general aside. Quite dismayed, he asked General Lee, "Don't you know the officer you're recommending is one of your biggest critics? Why, he never hesitates to undermine your policies and shows little respect for your position." General Lee answered calmly, "I know all this, but the president wanted my opinion of him, not his opinion of me."

Whenever we do achieve our goals, it is vital we use our success well. To maintain a positive attitude, we must not be vengeful and vindictive toward our current and former competitors. We must respect our adversaries, which in turn will keep us from becoming bitter. For bitterness is the mortal enemy of a great attitude.

Now for Churchill's last line, "In Peace, Goodwill." Champions have an attitude that shows goodwill toward others, based on respect for themselves. They believe that success and achievement should be theirs, and if another also succeeds, they are not intimidated. A positive attitude leaves no room for pettiness, slander, or ill will.

With all of this in mind, the salesperson should monitor his or her attitude frequently, keeping it on course with the guidelines previously discussed. Like Zig Zigler says, "We should, from time to time, take a check-up from the neck up," because before any action can be taken and have a chance to succeed, it must first start with a great, positive attitude.

FACT SIX: *Attitude must be influenced by reality-based action.*

In the year 1912 a majestic sight appeared on the coastline of Scotland. It was the newly constructed ocean liner *Titanic* on her maiden voyage bound for America. This was, to date, the world's greatest nautical achievement, and both the crew and the passengers held the conviction that she was the safest vessel ever built. In fact, everyone was so positive of the *Titanic's* invincibility that even the captain ignored a report sighting dangerous icebergs in the freezing North Atlantic. So with his positive attitude in place, the captain failed to slow down and at full speed steamed ahead. Then the unthinkable happened; the unsinkable *Titanic* was torn asunder after striking a huge iceberg. The *Titanic* sank taking with her fifteen hundred lives. The lesson to be learned here is a positive mental attitude is good, but only when it's tempered with reality-based action. Always be aware that a positive attitude by itself can become nothing but a gross deception. An attitude is simply a decision about what course of action you'll take when confronted with a set of circumstances. After this decision has been made, however, it can be implemented only by taking fact-related action. Regrettably, some people get the attitude part down right, but then fail to take the action needed to produce positive results. Likewise, we must be positive in selling, but this positive attitude must address the reality that nothing good will come to us without the action of hard work. As Will Rogers said, "Even if you're on the right track, you'll get run over if you just sit there." To be a winner in life, you've got to decide that enough is enough, that this time I'm going to turn on the afterburners and redline this thing called work. I'm going to give it everything I've got and soar past the average and ordinary. Here's the winning formula:

Positive Attitude + Facts + Action = Results

The truth about attitude is you're really not positive unless your attitude over time produces positive results. If it doesn't, your attitude is lacking depth and is merely a distortion of reality. So develop the right attitude plus the facts, and make sure you always take action. Contrary to some of the one-dimensional positive-attitude gurus, it's not enough to will the end, you've got to provide the means.

MAINTAINING YOUR WINNING ATTITUDE

Once you develop the right attitude, what's the best way to keep it? How does one stay positive despite the tremendous pressure at the top? A reporter once asked basketball mega-star Charles Barkley this very question, and he responded thoughtfully with a philosophy that mirrors my own. Barkley said that the reason he was so positive was because he "always concentrates on the negative first." Explaining this seeming paradox, he said, "Whenever I'm faced with a duty or situation I begin to resent, I quickly list the negative alternatives. So in dealing with excessive fan and media demands, I first think about the nasty consequences of *no* fan or media interest!"

Faithfully practiced, this exercise can help us all maintain a good attitude and perspective. This outlook is closely related to the idea that the easiest way to stay positive and contented is to regularly count your blessings. Likewise, the quickest way to develop a poor attitude is to ignore them.

EXERCISES

A. Become a student of great attitudes. Choose at least three heroes or heroines and read their various biographies. Also, study at least one book per month from the recommended reading list at the back of this book.

B. Analyze the soundness of your own attitude by reviewing the results it has achieved to this date. Try to discover patterns of success or failure.

C. Make yourself accountable to someone you respect who has reached the level you wish to attain.

2

COMPETITION:
THE PRINCIPLES OF WAR

*The biggest things are the easiest to do
because there's less competition.*
CORNELIUS VAN HORNE

It's said you have only two problems in sales. One is not making enough money and the other is someone making more than you. Most people have experienced the problem of not making enough money, but how many have given any thought to the second half of that statement which, in essence, deals with the issue of competition?

Certainly there's no argument that competition is a reality, but ultimately people compete to satisfy themselves. We set a personal goal and then judge our overall success by the progress we make toward achieving it. But sooner or later, life presents us with someone who outperforms even our best efforts. To protect our attitude and career we must be sure not to devalue ourselves while placing value on others. Remember, **your real competitor is easy to find: Just look in the mirror — it's been you all the time.**

But there are two sides to every coin. On one side are the perils inherent in devaluing ourselves when outperformed by others. On the other side is the danger of being on top and acting like it. Believing you are not as good as everyone else is bad; but believing you are better than everyone else is definitely worse.

We've all been taught the value of trying to be a "good loser." But not much is said about the importance of being a good winner. Truly, there are few situations in life more nauseating than having to tolerate a poor winner, yet many of us fall into this category when we experience even a hint of success. Benjamin Franklin described the root of the problem when he said, "In reality there is perhaps not one of our natural passions so hard to subdue as pride. Disguise it, struggle with it, beat it down, stifle it, mortify it as much as one pleases, it is still alive and, every now and then, will peek out and show itself. You will see it, perhaps often in this history, for even if I can conceive that I can completely overcome it, I should probably be proud of my humility." Franklin identifies the real culprit to poor sportsmanship: **The problem is pride.**

Unfortunately, the poor winner has become commonplace in today's world of business, sports, and entertainment. You know the type: self-centered braggadocios who are merciless in their opinions of others. I call it the #1 syndrome, and such people make poor role models, especially for our children! The main problem with poor winners is that they have become so prideful and conceited in their success that they serve no one but themselves. To their downfall, they usually make little provision to deal with a setback, which exemplifies the adage that pride does go before the fall. As Harry Truman observed, **"Conceit is God's gift to little men."** Am I saying that a person should be devoid of pride? Certainly not! For without pride, I'm afraid very little would be accomplished, as the following story proves.

Years ago Charles Schwab, Sr., was asked to help boost production in a factory that was dead last in Andrew Carnegie's sprawling steel empire. Others had tried and failed, but Schwab felt that he had the answer. Just before the day shift was to come in he took a big piece of chalk and inscribed on the floor a huge number 4. When the day shift workers came in they naturally asked what the 4 meant. They were told that that's how many production runs the night shift was able to get done. Well, the day shift wasn't to be outdone, and eight hours later, to everyone's surprise except Schwab, there was a big 5 emblazoned on the floor. This trend continued until production in the plant actually doubled in a very short time, illustrating that controlled pride and competition is a positive force but, like everything else, it must be tempered with practical goals and good sportsmanship.

COMPETITION

POINT 1: *Competition level = Commitment level.*

I've never met a person who willingly washed a rental car, nor have I heard of a kamikaze pilot being decorated for flying twenty missions. The problem in both of these cases can be traced to a lack of commitment. With the rental car and the expendable pilot, a lack of commitment is understandable, because both situations provide little benefit to the subject. So before there can be commitment, there has to be a perceived benefit. In other words, there has to be a "why" before there is a "will." People need to envision a reward before they commit. This is because the hardest part of achievement is the fact that you don't really know you can win until you do. This lack of certainty causes many people to hold back. They want a guarantee of success before they commit. This approach, however, gives their efforts no backbone and they become pussycat competitors, preferring to fold in the face of adversity rather than wager their all. You can compete only up to the level that you commit. Commitment, regardless of the potential outcome, must come first. To win you have to adopt the motto of the historic 82d Airborne Division, which simply states, **"ALL THE WAY."**

POINT 2: *Judge efforts, not performance.*

Just what is a healthy attitude toward competition? First, always judge your effort and not your performance. It's one thing to know we have been temporarily defeated and could have done much more to avoid failure. But it's quite another matter to know we did our best, yet came up a little short. In this, there's at least the satisfaction of knowing we did all we could. If at the end of the day you can say that you've done all you could possibly do and made a full effort, you're on the winning track. Even if the rewards may not have materialized, satisfaction and commitment will still be maintained and, over time, great effort will inevitably produce great performance.

POINT 3: *Always remember every dog has its day.*

The third point to remember in competing successfully is that every dog has its day. This saying was particularly soothing to me in some very trying times. As a manager in a large sales and marketing company, I found myself in direct competition with another individual who was a true competitor. Every month when the figures came in, it was either him or me who came out on top.

Then came a period of about a year and a half when his organization dramatically outproduced ours. Sadly, this success eventually went to his head. He began making derogatory statements about us and others. Things like, "They just can't cut it; they're not as good as us," or, "We'll always be #1, because the competition's a joke!" and the nail that sealed his coffin, "We'll never be defeated!" It's one thing to win, but quite another thing to flaunt success in an opponent's face.

Over time, things turned out differently than he expected. Our group rallied and became dominant and, to my surprise, this once-victorious, confident leader became completely disoriented, disenchanted, and broken. Fortunately, he bounced back, but it was a painful process. The point is, enjoy success, but understand that nothing goes on forever. When you're on top, enjoy it and strive to stay there, but if you should fall back down, don't let it destroy your career. Life is a series of ups and downs. Be prepared for both journeys.

POINT 4: *Always leave a defeated opponent a way out.*

The truly victorious are the ones who try to elevate those they have just defeated. We should always be careful that we don't turn vanquished competitors into lifelong, mortal enemies. It's imperative to never belittle competitors, but rather treat them with respect and dignity. If we win, great; we're the best that day. Insulting opponents and publicly humiliating them is unsportsmanlike and only produces bitter enemies. Better to win graciously and fairly and have the respect of opponents, than to garner their contempt with bad form. Leave that to our friends in professional wrestling, where it's all theatrics, isn't it?

Smart salespeople are keenly aware of the need for competition, because it fuels the fires of success. But they're also aware of the fact that an uncontrolled fire can consume everything in its wake. Competition is a flame that must be fanned, but it must never be allowed to consume the goodwill and spirit of cooperation needed to make a business run successfully. Always leave your opponents a way out. Compete and defeat them, yes, but allow them some way to save face. Failing to do this is like slapping a rattlesnake after you capture it. There's really no need, and it just invites trouble.

POINT 5: *Concentrate on what you can do to the competition.*

The fifth point to consider when competing is to always concentrate on what you can do to the competition, not what the competition can do to you. In studying the greatest generals of military history, you'll find one great similarity, and it's not their background, education, height, race, or age. The most distinguishing mark of the great generals is the fact they didn't worry about what the opposing force would do to them so much as what they would do to the opposing force. Napoleon Bonaparte gave special credence to this point when he said, **"He who fears being conquered is sure of defeat."**

The same is true of great salespeople. They don't become bogged down with fear of what the competition will do to them so much as focus on what they will achieve over the competition. In war, sports, and sales, the best defense is always a great offense. Never forget that to be a champion you must first be a great competitor, always willing to take the battle to the opponent. This takes a special quality.

In sports coaches witness many players who possess tremendous skill. Some of these players perform flawlessly in practice yet, strangely, in a game situation their performance is less than inspiring. On the other hand, coaches also see players who aren't nearly so talented and yet they possess something unique which comes alive during a game. This factor helps them rise to a level of play they may never have reached before. These special people truly have the competitive spirit. They have what's known as the **killer instinct,** and this instinct helps them win, sometimes against great odds. I am reminded of a story in which a courageous Chihuahua took on a Great Dane in a life-and-death struggle. When it was all over, the Chihuahua emerged tattered but victorious. The Great Dane's owner arrived late at the scene, not having witnessed the fight. Confused, he tearfully asked an old bystander how this could have happened. The bystander hemmed and hawed a bit and then said, "Well, as I see it, your dog must have choked himself to death trying to swallow that dadgum Chihuahua." The point is no matter how improbable, **a winner will find a way to win!**

POINT 6: *Every knock's a boost.*

You probably realize that not everyone you compete against is going to play fair. In fact, what's unfair to you may be perfectly acceptable to your opponent. That's why you should never be surprised when you're dealt a low blow. This blow may be a vicious attack on your character or a slanderous charge against your company. Whatever it is, try to immediately go on the offensive, but remember to stay calm because no one is ever as mad as the one who is wrong. Never attack who they are, but always attack what they do by showing that you can do it better. Concentrate your offense on products and concepts, not people and characters, and make sure you do this truthfully and with class. Remember, smear campaigns directed against you will eventually backfire, especially when they begin with a false premise. All this accomplishes is to create interest, and if you're right, this interest will eventually vindicate you and then help you to succeed. The chain of events usually follows this order:

First, **persecution:**	Wrongful assault based on falsehood or distortions.
Second, **protection:**	Vindication over time by the truth.
Third, **promotion:**	Victory, restoration, and even gain as the perpetrator is discredited by the facts.

If you're right and you fight, every knock's a boost in the long run! "Don't worry about the Pygmies, just keep cutting a path."

In the final analysis, the great salespeople embrace competition. They must truly love to compete and be able to rise to any challenge and get the job done in spite of the opposition! They are also wise enough to temper their competitive nature with common sense and fair play, keeping a focus on their long-term goals. Smart salespeople keep success and competition in the right perspective.

If you ever have the chance to go to Wimbledon and watch that grand old tennis tournament, the highlight is always when the finalists make their way onto the center court to battle for the title. Just before they reach center court the champions have to pass through a doorway. Above this hallowed portal is written a quote, which perhaps reveals the essence of maintaining consistent performance and competing successfully. It's from Rudyard Kipling's poem "If" and it issues to the combatants a thoughtful statement to ponder: **"If you can meet with triumph and disaster and treat those two impostors just the same, then you'll be a man my son."** What a great truth to consider when we're faced with competition!

POINT 7: *Know your real enemy.*

Believe it or not, your real enemies are seldom your competition. Yes, they're your rival and often a thorn in your side, but like yourself they're combatants in a legitimate contest. Like you they share a dream and are engaged in this pursuit with every fiber of their existence. They aren't the real enemy, but rather a reflection of yourself to be contended with on the road to victory. The real enemy is not the dreamer who approaches the dream from a different perspective. **The real enemies are the dream stealers who have given up and can justify their actions only by convincing others to do the same.** These vile creatures are the true threat that you must constantly guard against. I once heard it said that there are three types of people: the searcher, the skeptic, and the scorner. The first two are the believers, with the skeptic cautiously needing more facts to be convinced. The third, however, is devoid of belief and seeks to destroy anything associated with it. This bankrupt type is the true adversary, who will seek to suck the faith from a dreamer like a Transylvanian vampire. You can recognize this group because they are the mockers, the abusive, and the lowest form of enemy: the traitor. From these, flee.

HOW TO COMPETE AGAINST THE BEST AND WIN

On the road to success you'll often be faced with very formidable opponents. These supercompetitors can be found both inside and outside your company. The tendency is to look at the accomplishments of these great achievers and then at your own track record, which may, at the time, pale by comparison. Looking at the big picture this way can be quite intimidating and unconducive to good performance. A better approach is to attack the problem on a smaller scale. It's the old "how to eat an elephant" philosophy. One bite at a time. **To attack the biggest and the best, make up your mind to beat them at the little things first.** I call this the "one step beyond" tactic.

One Step Beyond   For instance, if the superachievers get to the office at 7:30 A.M., you get there at 7:25. If they work overtime, you work slightly more overtime. If they are just listening at a business meeting, you be sure to take detailed notes. If they call their clients to thank them for business, make sure you call your clients and also send a personal thank-you note. Actions like these may seem small and insignificant, but they serve an important psychological function. They instill in you piece by piece the experience and knowledge that your largest competitors are not superhuman and can be beaten!

Once you have gained confidence in the little things, you can tackle the big ones and compete on a larger scale. To do this, first mimic your competitor's every action, again doing it one step beyond. If you find out that they see six prospects per day, do the same but add one or two more. Over time, an extra effort like this will yield positive results, and before you know it you'll be performing on or above the level of your competition. Another factor in giant killing is taking advantage of the fact that most titans sooner or later will pause, rest, or hesitate in their performance. When this happens, you will get your best chance at passing them. Be patient and persistent, and at some point your competitors will blink. When they do, turn on the afterburners and assume the lead. Then remember what Grand Slam tennis champion Rod Laver once said: **"The time your game is most vulnerable is when you're ahead; never let up."**

Avoid Rationalization

Top athletes who have turned in a poor performance don't rationalize it away; instead they put in extra time on the practice field. They purposely punish themselves to stay at a high level of performance. To compete with the best, you must apply this same principle in sales. You can't rationalize away poor production. So if you don't reach your weekly or monthly sales goal, punish yourself by working weekends and overtime. This may be unthinkable to the average corporate salesperson, but that's why they're average and often expendable. If you don't punish yourself for subpar performance, you can soon rationalize yourself right out of the business. **Beware of rationalization, it's the breakfast of losers.**

The Power of the Push

Like the great generals, successful salespeople use the power of the push. Whether as an individual or as a member of a group, increasing performance level is mostly a question of breaking down barriers. Once one has been breached, it becomes easier to do it again and again. The easiest way to break down barriers is to challenge yourself with regularly timed pushes. A push is a short period of time, say thirty to sixty days, in which you work at your fullest mental, physical, and emotional capacity. This is done to reach a specific goal. Of course, when you break this goal you award yourself abundantly. Needless to say, you'll be surprised at just how much you can accomplish with this kind of self-imposed pressure. So plan two or three major pushes per year and force your performance to a higher level. At first glance, competing with the best can be intimidating, but if you break it down into smaller steps success becomes attainable. All you need to do is win in the small things first, mimic your competitors, go one step beyond, and utilize the awesome power of the push.

THE PLAID PERSPECTIVE

Keeping a competitive edge requires balanced attention in a number of areas of life. Serious neglect in any one area will lead to less than effective performance. To help you monitor these areas, you simply need to adopt the Plaid Perspective (see Figure 2.1).

Power The possession of control, authority, and influence in business starts with our ability to harness power within ourselves, which manifests itself in three ways: spiritually, physically, and mentally. Monitoring our lives in the following ways will ensure a vigorous and positive outlook.

Spiritual: Maintaining our relationship with the Creator.

Physical: Keeping our bodies healthy through exercise, diet, and rest.

Mental: Developing our minds intellectually and emotionally through positive input.

POWER	*Spiritual, physical, and mental*
LOVE	*Fulfilling the needs of others first*
ADAPTABILITY	*Embracing change*
IMAGINATION	*Dreaming, goal setting, and organization*
DEEDS	*Drive, determination and the guts to finish what you start*

FIGURE 2.1   The Plaid Perspective

Love   The word *love* helps us keep in mind that to win in business and in our personal life, we need to show positive emotion and fulfill the needs of others first.

Adaptability   This is a trigger word that challenges us to embrace positive change, continue to grow, and avoid falling into ruts. Being adaptable keeps us open-minded and sensitive to new solutions.

Imagination   Take time to dream. Walt Disney called his dreamers "imagineers," and they were the most important people in his organization. You have to be the imagineer of your own life **because your dreams are the path away from your problems and toward your destiny.** Dreaming helps us set goals, make plans, and get organized.

Deeds   Just north of Michigan you'll find a busy little Canadian town called Glencoe, which was named by its pioneering Scottish founders. Here in a small churchyard rest my Munro ancestors. Inscribed on one of the weathered headstones is this thoughtful epitaph:

> *Remember man as you walk by*
> *As you are now so once was I*
> *As I am now soon you will be*
> *So prepare for death and follow me.*

Some may think that's morbid, but it doesn't change the fact that we're not here for long. It makes no sense not to urgently turn our dreams into reality through our deeds. Action and the guts to finish what we've started are the final element in the Plaid Perspective. Committed to memory and used regularly, this outlook on life will keep you balanced, happy, and competitive.

EXERCISES

A. Spend five minutes each day vividly remembering your own victories and achievements. Think of how you felt, what you saw, and what you heard at the time. Now envision yourself in the same vivid detail accomplishing and winning in your current pursuit.

B. Commit to memory this line: Failure is but apprenticeship to great victories. Failure is part of my plan. It makes me better, tougher, and more committed to winning!

C. Take time to evaluate your current game plan. Keep in mind, **never change a game plan that's winning** and never keep one that's not.

3

EMOTION: THE POWERFUL CATALYST TO ACTION

Never forget the most powerful force on earth is love.
NELSON ROCKEFELLER TO HENRY KISSINGER

First came the use of fire. Then came the invention of the wheel. Next came the revelation that selling is an emotional experience. I only wish someone would have told me, but, alas, eventually I found out. It happened early in my career. I had just come back from a call and was relating to my colleague, Paul, what had transpired. Paul was a real character who always referred to himself as 165 pounds of romping, stomping romance. Anyway, see if this story doesn't sound familiar.

I was telling my peer, with great animation, that I couldn't believe the client I had just seen didn't buy. I explained that I had worked on this sale for weeks and had compiled an arsenal of indisputable facts and figures to back up my detailed proposal. The need was there and the price was right. In fact, this client would have saved thousands of dollars if they had bought! But they didn't. I was frustrated, dejected, and downright angry. I couldn't believe it! Then this veteran salesperson said something that changed my thinking about selling entirely. Paul asked me, "Did you just show features or did you sell benefits? Did you concentrate on the steak or did you describe the sizzle?" Well, I thought about this for a while and afterward came to realize what Paul was getting at: **People don't always buy because things make sense, but people buy because of what they sense.**

I began to see that although your product must have a logical foundation to be saleable, people won't necessarily buy it unless they experience an emotional response to it. In other words, **sales are conceived with logic, but made on emotion.**

WHY PEOPLE CHANGE

This led me to think in-depth about which was more powerful, logic or emotion? I quickly came to the conclusion that emotion is by far the more powerful of the two. Psychologists tell us that most people will not change unless they have a powerful emotional experience to instigate that change. In looking at people uncondemningly, this appears to be true. For instance, I know many people who still smoke. Logically, they know the grim statistics and potential consequences of smoking, but day after day and year after year they continue to smoke. Then suddenly comes a heart attack and immediately they quit smoking. The power of logic was ineffectual but the emotion of fear had an immediate effect, and a change of behavior was made.

I then began to wonder which was the most powerful emotion of all. Not surprisingly, the answer I found was love. This powerful emotion provides us with the greatest feeling of comfort and overall self-worth. The fact is no other emotion is so powerpacked. In a sense this can be viewed as logical, because scripture tells us God is love and the last I heard, God is still considered to be the most powerful force there is. Of course, for this logic to work, it helps to believe in the possibility of a scriptural God.

You know, it's funny. Initially, I thought fear might be the most powerful of emotions because it's so hard to control. But I couldn't help thinking of all the stories of wartime valor, where men and women sacrificed themselves unselfishly for others. I also thought of a mother's love and how most mothers would gladly die to save their baby's life. It's truly unbelievable what the desire to love and to be loved will do. It will compel people to punish themselves unmercifully in a gym to build a body that may get them attention, and hopefully love. It will also spur a musician or an artist to practice and suffer rejection in order to gain the ultimate prize of fame, which is, in a sense, the love of others for what you do. Love will, in effect, keep people working faithfully in a job they bitterly dislike because they want to provide a good environment for the family they love. The fact is, most of what we accomplish in life is because of strong emotional motivation, with love leading the list.

What does all this have to do with selling? Well, just that all of our fantastic product knowledge and computer-generated facts are useless unless they affect our clients emotionally. It becomes readily apparent that if we want to succeed in sales we must first understand the power of emotion, and purposely appeal to that power in our endeavors. **We have to cater not only to the intellect, but to the harbor of the emotions, the heart.**

With this settled, the question then becomes, How best do we stimulate our clients' emotions? The answer is quite simple — by using another emotion: *excitement*. Ralph Waldo Emerson was right when he said, "Nothing great is accomplished without enthusiasm." **The use of emotion is the catalyst to action.** But how much emotion should we use?

E2L1 — THE THEORY OF SALEABILITY

Of course, it's one thing to accept the impact of emotion; but finding the right amount to use in selling is quite another matter. What's the right mix of emotion to logic? I've developed a simple formula which can be easily taught and practiced by anyone, with good results. (I was going to call it the Munro Doctrine, but I didn't want to get it confused with that president who spelled his name wrong.)

The secret formula is **E2L1,** which means 2 parts emotion to each part logic. Along with these proportions, it's important to utilize them in the proper order and with specific purpose.

For example, if you're introducing a certain feature of a product to a customer, you open with 1 part emotion. This would be an emotion-based statement creating curiosity and interest for the feature. Next, you present the logic part, which is the feature itself. Finally, you close with the second part of emotion. This is another emotional statement, this time highlighting a benefit of the feature. This is the "what's in it for the customer" part.

Okay, let's put this all together with a practical example. Suppose I was selling men's suits and wanted to familiarize a customer with the high grade of fabric used. Holding the suit, I would open with one part of emotion, creating interest.

Salesperson: Jim, look at this. This is something exciting to see.
Customer: What?

Next I use logic to explain the feature.

Salesperson: Just look and feel this genuine Irish wool weave. It comes from sheep fed only Guiness beer and hand-sheared using Swiss army knives.
Customer: Hey, that feels great!

Now I add my second emotion, which unveils the benefit.

Salesperson: It not only feels great, but imagine how
good you'll feel wearing it. I don't think
anything looks as good to others as old-fashioned quality.

That's E2L1 —the Theory of Saleability! 2 parts emotion
sandwiching 1 part logic.

HOT-BUTTON – LIST SELLING USING E2L1

John Wesley, the legendary speaker and founder of the
Methodist Church, expressed his formula for creating
interest this way. He said, "First I set myself on fire, and
then the people come to watch me burn."

The smart salesperson realizes everything starts with
you. Before you can expect someone to be excited about
your product, you have to be excited about it yourself. In
order to be enthusiastic about what I'm selling, I find it
helpful to make a special list, which I call a hot-button
list. You merely write down everything that excites you
about what you're selling and how it helps others. After
you've finished your list, tape it to your appointment
book and read it faithfully, ideally before every appointment. This allows you to start every presentation on a
positive basis, using the catalyst of your own excitement.
If you want to start a fire, you do it by introducing another flame. In sales, if you want someone to be fired up
about what you offer, you have to ignite yourself first. It's
simple, but many salespeople nevertheless try to sell
armed only with facts and figures and no emotional fire.

By composing a hot-button list you can stay focused
on what excites you about your product. Once you're
excited, it becomes much easier to excite the client during
the initial stages of the presentation. This sets a positive
tone and atmosphere for everything else that follows.

Finding Your Client's Hot Buttons

Once you're enthusiastic about your product, the next step is to discover what excites the client. It will probably be something quite different from your own motivation. This investigation will be accomplished by asking questions and carefully listening to what the client tells you. In this, try to follow the **30/70 rule.** That is, the salesperson should speak 30 percent of the time and listen to the client 70 percent of the time. This gives clients a chance to reveal their needs and interests. And once you find out what the client is excited about, you immediately shift your excitement to it!

For example, suppose I was selling luxury automobiles. At the start of my day while I review my appointment book, I might also read over my hot-button list. Reading my list reminds me just what excites me about these cars. It tells me, for instance, that I love to be around well-designed and finely engineered automobiles. I like knowing just how they work and all their specifications. I also get a thrill relating my knowledge of cars to others. Now, after reading my hot-button list, I meet my first prospects. They're husband and wife, and it's not hard for them to see the enthusiasm I have for the car they're looking at. So I'm off to a positive start. Through questions I'll seek some common ground and discover their interest, or hot button. After asking where they're from and trying to find a connection, I ask, "Mr. and Mrs. Prospect, just out of curiosity, what do you think is the most important feature to look for in an automobile?" The husband speaks up, saying it's performance and reliability. With this I'll begin using E2L1 and tell them about the twenty-four-valve engine, dependability, and fuel economy. I end this segment emotionally by saying how respected this vehicle is by the automobile world and how people who choose it are thought of as well-informed buyers. I then offer them a test drive. The husband nods his head in agreement, but appears reserved. Fortunately I happened to have overheard the wife tell him that she likes the plush interior of this model and feels this car would be safer and more comfortable than their current vehicle.

Great! She has just disclosed two more hot buttons. One is the luxury of the interior, which is basically connected with the emotion of pride. The second is the safety and comfort, which deals with our emotional need to protect and care for those we love.

I now have two options. First, I could ignore what she said and carry on, telling them about the reliability of the product, or I could immediately transfer my excitement and focus on the emotional hot buttons my client has just revealed. Of course, the second option is the best course, and from here on out I concentrate all my excitement and emphasis there, again using E2L1 to help the clients satisfy their interest.

The E2L1 Hot-Button Selling System Recap

1. Read your personal hot-button list, piquing your interest. (Hit your own hot buttons.)
2. Discover what the clients are excited about, using questions and observations. (Discover the clients' hot buttons.)
3. Shift your emphasis and excitement to the clients' hot buttons using E2L1. (Hit clients' hot buttons repeatedly.)
4. Satisfy clients' interests. (Help clients fulfill their hot-button needs.)

I can hear some of you saying, "Well, I can do the logic part, but I'm not the emotional type. I don't get excited." The fact is we're *all* highly emotional; some of us just don't show our emotions as readily as others. But

we are all motivated by our emotions. In fact, even the
behavior of not showing emotion is motivated by emotion
— the fear of looking foolish or being vulnerable. The
point of this armchair psychology is that emotion is an
effective tool the professional salesperson utilizes.

HOW TO SHOW EMOTION

It's not good enough to be emotional, you must learn to
show it. Take the emotion of love; it can't be fully experienced unless you can express it to someone else. It's not
good enough to just love your spouse, you have to be able
to express your love. The same holds true for excitement.
It's not enough to be excited about what you sell, you've
got to be able to convey that excitement.

For most salespeople, showing excitement is not a big
problem. For others, however, it is a skill that must be
acquired. If you happen to feel you need help showing
more emotion, don't worry; no matter what your disposi-
tion is now, with time you can change. There was a time
when I believed a man who told me he was the reserved
type and couldn't change. After personally witnessing
some remarkable transformations, however, I've decided
that much of a person's nature is merely habit, and habits
can be changed. It all comes down to *wanting* to change,
which reminds me of the old Marine Corps saying, **"I
can't really means I won't!"**

The following are some proven techniques that can
help transform your ability to convey excitement and
show emotion.

Imitation and Emulation

After desire, imitation is probably the first step toward
learning to express emotion. In looking at some very suc-

cessful personalities, it's remarkable to find how many started their careers sadly deficient in the area of showing emotion. General George S. Patton, for instance, felt he appeared timid and uninteresting, so he practiced faithfully in front of a mirror, imitating what he thought a "blood and guts" general should act like. He emulated the tough generals he idolized as a youth. Initially this new manner was unnatural to Patton, but he spent hours consciously imitating their more animated styles. Because of this, what was once unnatural became second nature. Needless to say, it worked. The name Patton is now synonymous with tough leadership. This is an important point, for no matter what you do, whether it's a golf swing, a tennis stroke, or when you first make a change it will probably feel alien and uncomfortable. But not to worry —psychologists tell us it takes sixty days to break a habit but only thirty days to make a new one.

This principle also holds true if you are trying to add more emotion to your presentation. At first you will be acting, and it won't feel natural. But after a short time it will be automatic and will feel as though you've always functioned this way.

In order to start this process, you must have something — or should I say someone — to imitate; you'll need to find a good role model. This could be the top salesperson in your company or someone else very successful in sales. Once you have chosen your role model, your next task is to mimic his or her every move. You might want to videotape a sales presentation and learn it word for word, gesture for gesture. **Remember, body language is just as important as words, accounting for an estimated 55 percent of communication.** Oh, and don't worry about being unoriginal. After you have learned and mastered your role model's presentation, you will naturally adapt and alter it, incorporating your own style. Imitating someone else doesn't make you unoriginal, it merely augments your own originality.

Emphasis

One very important aspect of conveying emotion is the use of emphasis. It's remarkable how, by emphasizing a few select adjectives, you can inject tremendous excitement into your presentation. To illustrate this, compose a sentence using a powerful adjective, for example, "this product is revolutionary." Say the proceeding sentence using no emphasis at all. Now emphasize the revolutionary, making this word stand out in your speech. This simple technique makes a big difference in conveying extra emotion. Try to become a master at invigorating your sales presentation by emphasizing select adjectives. Keep in mind that these adjectives should be contemporary and meaningful; avoid hackneyed terms like *incredible* or *awesome*. Always have a smile in your voice and don't overdo it. Remember, it's not so much *what* you say as *how you say it* that counts.

Volume

I once asked a person I admired how to show more excitement. He quickly responded by saying, **"You should talk louder and walk faster."** I haven't figured out how to incorporate the "walk faster" part, unless you can talk to your clients on a treadmill. But the idea of talking louder intrigued me and, after studying successful salespeople, I found that most do talk loudly, however not all the time; increased volume works best in small doses. Also — and I say this loud and clear — when I say talk loudly, I'm not referring to the decibel output of a top fuel dragster, but rather any increase in volume above normal. It's related to emphasis — using volume to drive your main points home. Truly, there is nothing worse than listening to someone speaking in a monotone. All this produces is boredom, and, as we all know, this is grounds for shooting someone in most southern states!

The Hypnotic Effect of Pause and Rhythm

When studying the speech patterns of people with extraordinary selling skill, be aware of their use of pace and rhythm. The pace or tempo at which great salespeople speak usually follows a set pattern and has developed its own rhythm, which is denoted by undulations in volume, pitch, and speed. All these factors in the right combination create a pleasant, almost hypnotic, effect. **I like to call this the snake-charmer effect.** Although this may be sophisticated stuff, if you're aware of it you'll be able to imitate it and develop your own personal style. You should also make use of one of the most powerful tools of language — *the pause.* The pause capitalizes on one of the great physical laws of nature which, to paraphrase, states: nature despises a vacuum and will always give top priority to its elimination. Used properly in speaking, the pause will create a similar effect on your listeners, making them extremely attentive. By using the language tools of rhythm, pace, and pause in your speaking, you will polish and perfect your persuasive style.

The Italian scholar and poet Petrarch put it beautifully when he said, **"Sameness is the mother of disgust, variety the cure."** By introducing into our presentations the use of imitation, emphasis, and changes in volume, pitch, and pace, we will keep ourselves and our prospects keenly interested in what we say. There's just no excuse for being uninteresting.

Phoney Hype Versus Heartfelt Belief

Let's tackle a perpetual argument against the use of emotion in sales. You've probably heard this one as many times as you've heard politicians say, "no new taxes." This argument goes like this: "I don't get emotional because I don't believe in using all that phoney hype." We're glad to hear it, because neither does the extraordinary salesperson. Hype is usually exaggeration designed to convince someone to do something that will, most often, only benefit the person doing the hyping. Hype does not necessarily work from the basis of truth, so it is worlds apart from what we are talking about. When we speak of using emotion in sales, it's to help express a heartfelt belief that will benefit not just ourselves but others as well. Our emotion, in this case, is based entirely on truth. Hype motivation is a scheme from the mind, but emotional motivation comes from the heart. You should never confuse the two.

Your Excitement Barometer

Everyone operates at a different level of emotional intensity. For some, it will be necessary to raise this level to increase their overall success in selling. For others, however, it may be advisable to tone down their emotions. From taking medicine to putting curb feelers on a Mercedes, you can have too much of a good thing. Not enough emotion will bore people; too much can outright scare them. The right level to maintain is probably just a little higher than your average client's attitude, enough to comfortably get their attention and keep it. So adjust your excitement barometer accordingly. See Figure 3.1.

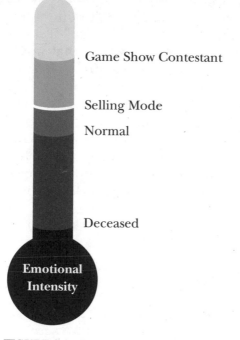

Game Show Contestant

Selling Mode

Normal

Deceased

Emotional
Intensity

FIGURE 3.1 Your Excitement Barometer

Sensory Focus

As humans we all take in and process information to help
navigate our world. The concept of sensory focus believes,
however, that people don't process information by using the
same senses. For example, some people may rely more heav-
ily on **visual** pictures to help them gain meaning. Others
may rely on **kinesthetics** or feelings to make sense of things.
Still others are more **auditory** in their analysis. What this
means to us in sales is that to trigger the right emotional
response and understanding, we may have to adapt our
words to the specific type of stimulus our customers will respond to. For instance, if a customer uses phrases like "I
hear you" or "That sounds fine," they probably respond

best to auditory stimulus. In this case you would mimic their phraseology by saying things like, "How does that sound to you" or "I hear you loud and clear." If a customer uses phrases like "I can't see where that would work" or "I see what you mean" they're probably more visual and you would respond likewise with phrases like "Get the picture" or "In my view this works best." The kinesthetic person will use words like "I feel good about this" or "This doesn't feel right." Here you would craft your speech to describe feelings by saying things like "This is a feature you can really warm up to" or "Going this route is a hard road." It's attention to these details in our speech that separates the extraordinary from the mediocre.

A Willingness to Change

As discussed previously, emotion is a powerful force in selling, and the prudent salesperson will make sure this force is fully understood. Likewise, the smart salesperson also knows that long-term success in selling is directly linked to the ability to change. Most of us are not born to greatness, we have to evolve to it. Winston Churchill is considered one of the greatest orators of our time, but in his initial speaking performance to the British Parliament he showed only a pale shadow of the eloquence he later exhibited during the war years. Churchill clearly saw the need to change and he worked on his speeches endlessly. He was especially meticulous in practicing his delivery until what he said carried the emotion and emphasis required to bolster his nation against a life-threatening foe.

Another great portrait in change is Theodore Roosevelt, one of America's most powerful and best-loved presidents. Very early in his career as a young assemblyman in New York, he was laughed out of the legislature after making his first speech. No one had seen anything quite like Teddy before. His style was so different, his manner clumsy and abrupt. Roosevelt, though, was not discouraged by this initial failure, and he worked hard to become one of the most original and convincing speakers in presidential history.

The point of all this is that if Winston Churchill, Theodore Roosevelt, Gen. George Patton, and other men and women of high caliber had to make dramatic changes in their modes of self-expression, you also should be willing to change in order to reach your goals.

THE PLAID PERSONALITY PROFILE

With this background in mind, let's add a basic character study to help identify and better relate emotionally to the various types of prospects you'll meet in your sales career. To stay in theme for easy recollection, we use the Plaid Personality Profile (see Figure 3.2) to outline the major personality types. These personality types are denoted on the Plaid Grid (see Figure 3.3).

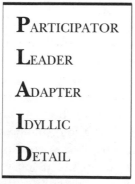

PARTICIPATOR

LEADER

ADAPTER

IDYLLIC

DETAIL

FIGURE 3.2 The Plaid Personality Profile

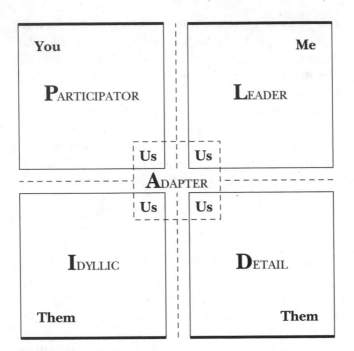

FIGURE 3.3   The Plaid Grid

Participator

These folks are easy to spot. They are extroverted and love any chance to socialize. They are experts at building and keeping personal relationships. These individuals love to be around people, and much of their motivation in life comes from their perceptions of how others see them. They are great team players. Their strengths are their diplomacy and desire to please others, which make them extremely popular. On the other hand, their weakness is pointed out by the word YOU in the top-left corner of the Participator grid. This indicates that on the negative side they sometimes tend to be overly concerned with what YOU or others think of them. This can inhibit them to the degree that they are easily influenced by flattery and tend to shy away from controversial decisions. When participators are frustrated or angry, they tend to be defensive and hurt and then go on the offensive. The participator's guiding desire is to be accepted and liked by others. Any selling must be directed to satisfying that need. To sell a participator, you should be relationship conscious.

Leader

These are the doers, the folks often found in management and ownership. They tend to be impatient, they like change, and they are always eager to take control of a situation. Their strengths are their drive for accomplishment and ability to make decisions. Their main motivation is to achieve and be in charge. Their inherent weakness is denoted by the word ME in the top-right corner of the Leader grid. ME signifies leaders who, at their worst, can be callous and domineering to others. When frustrated or angry, the leader type will generally become offensive and hostile. Their greatest fear is lack of control. Selling these folks is easy if you can get them involved to the extent that they are in control and the purchase is all their idea.

Adapter

The adapter is not a true personality type so much as a mode of behavior. Adapters choose to neutralize their own character and take on the attributes of the person they are dealing with. By this technique the adapter hopes to help each personality type feel comfortable enough to move to the middle of the grid to the word US, representing trust and balance. US is the win-win position.

For example, say I was a leader selling to a participator type. Rather than act like a leader and take control, I would adapt my style to that of my client. I would concentrate on selling to the participator type's needs, foremost of which is the desire to be accepted by others. I would concentrate on building a relationship, all the time assuring that the purchase would be applauded by other people. In this way, I have adapted. If I were a participator type selling to a leader, on the other hand, I would adapt by putting less emphasis on personal relationships and more on the benefits my product has to offer. After this, if interest has been generated, I would allow the leader to take control and ask all the questions about details that I purposely left out of my presentation. I would not sell the leader on the idea that others would admire the purchase so much as on the idea that the purchase would help him better achieve his goals. The adapter has the ability to perceive the personality type of the customer and change to meet these needs. **The adapter is a chameleon who changes to suit the environment.**

Idyllic

The word *idyll* means a poetic work suggesting a peaceful pastoral life or setting. The idyllic person is a very likable, security-conscious individual. They don't embrace change and place high value on comfort, home, and family. Idyllic folks represent a number of occupations, such as skilled laborers, accountants, clerks, draftsmen, entry-level managers, and computer personnel. These people are the backbone of the world and are easy to recognize. They're the ones who have been employed at the same job for years and years. The idyllic personality usually avoids conflict. They have strong views but are not outwardly opinionated. When frustrated or angry, they become defensive and withdrawn. They don't particularly like salespeople. Nor do they like risk, because risk invites the possibility of change to their secure lives. Their strengths are their common sense and dependability. Their weakness is represented by the word THEM in the Idyllic grid, which indicates that the idyllic person can be narrow-minded and overly cautious, feeling if THEY, meaning the world, would just quit trying to change things, everything would be fine. The idyllic person's overriding fear, which must be consistently addressed during a sales presentation, is of losing security. As an adapter I would sell these folks by showing them that any purchase made would strengthen and enhance their overall security and comfort.

Detail

This is an important group, for without them we would not have buildings, bridges, airplanes, or anything else that relies upon precise planning and exactness of design. Some professions included in the detail group are doctors, architects, scientists, computer analysts, and the engineering sector. The detail person is driven by a need to perform to perfection. Most detail-oriented people are highly organized and despise anyone who isn't. The detail person finds security and comfort in facts and figures and precise modes of operation. They are goal oriented, but sometimes tend to be overanalytical, dwelling more on how something works than the fact that it does work. Their strengths are in their consistency and attention to detail. Their weakness is usually a lack of people skills. Again the word THEM in their grid denotes a downside: detailers sometimes can be perfectionists to the degree that it becomes difficult to work with them. The word THEM indicates that the detail person may sometimes feel that if others would just stick to the facts and quit acting on emotion, the world would be a better place. When frustrated or angry, the detail person can be unreasonable and aggressive. Their greatest fear is making a mistake by taking action without having all the facts. The Civil War general, George B. McClellan, is a classic example of a detail person paralyzed by this fear. Although a brilliant tactition, McClellan eventually had to be replaced as Union commander because of his inability to take action. As an adapter, you should be patient with detail prospects and make sure you give them all the facts they require. Also, to help put them at ease, you should learn the lingo of their field of business. This will immediately win their respect. During the selling process, the adapter must consistently assure the detail person of the sound logic involved in owning the product. An adapter must be a truly strong closer to help the detail person buy. The detailer must know that any emotional need is justified by the facts. Perhaps the best formula to sell a detailer is E2L2, using twice as much logic.

There you have the four main personality types and the adapter mode. Keep in mind that the personality profile shown is broad based. People are never composed of just one personality type, rather, we are a mixture of all types, with an overall dominant theme. For instance, you could be a participator but also have a high degree of leader and a moderate degree of detail qualities. The combinations are endless. Instinctively you probably already know or can guess your overall personality type. As a further point of interest in relationships, you will generally have the easiest time relating to those personality types touching your grid on the immediate left or right.

Example: participator and leader. The second easiest group to relate to will be those directly on the top or bottom of your grid.

Example: detail and leader. Those behavioral styles offering the most conflict are those diametrically opposite your grid. For instance, the detail person may have little tolerance for the participator, who is more emotional.

The participator, on the other hand, can't fathom why the detail person is so cold and uninterested in socializing. The leader and the idyllic types are also diametrically opposed and have similar conflict potential, with the idyllic person sometimes resenting the leader's love of change and action, and the leader not understanding the idyllic love of routine.

All this makes life interesting, to say the least. It also alerts us to the fact that treating our prospects as though they were all the same type of person with the same needs is a very simpleminded and disastrous approach to selling. With the Plaid Personality Profile, you will be better able to understand your prospects and appeal to their needs in a precise and appropriate manner.

In conclusion, **successful salespeople will actively develop the ability to show their feelings and emotions, which gives their sales presentations a special quality and sincerity.** They will also be sensitive to the emotional temperament of their prospects, adapting their behavior to meet the needs of others.

EXERCISES

A. Practice becoming a public speaker. There is no better forum for learning the art of connecting emotionally with other people.

B. Memorize the strengths, weaknesses, and desires of each personality type. Learn to adapt and relate to each.

4

SELF-PROMOTION: WINNING THE PEOPLE GAME

*Public sentiment is everything, with it nothing
can fail, without it nothing can succeed.*
ABRAHAM LINCOLN

Ted Turner, the colorful cable television visionary of
CNN, once said, "The key to success is get up early, go to
bed late, work like hell and advertise, advertise, advertise." Successful salespeople understand the truth in Mr.
Turner's statement, especially the emphasis he placed on
the role of advertising, or in our case, **self-promotion.**

It's common knowledge that any commodity will benefit
from promotion, but most people limit the importance
of promotion to cars, coffee, and detergent. To rise to
the highest levels in your sales career, however, it's imperative that you expand your use of advertising to include
yourself. After all, you're a commodity, and probably the
only one you have total control over. Like any other product, you will only succeed if people know and want what
you have to offer. That's where the art of self-promotion
comes into play.

For the record, I'll admit I had some reservations
about writing about self-promotion. After all, there seems

to be too much attention put on the self these days. But if we start from the premise that **self-promotion can be accomplished only by serving and elevating others,** we should be all right.

Of course, in talking about self-promotion, there is always the danger some misguided individual will feel that this alone is the answer to success. It's not! Self-promotion can work only if all the other steps to success, like hard work, dedication, and persistence, have been taken.

Like other products, you'll be used only if you perform. Self-promotion can help get you noticed, but you had better have the goods to merit that attention. Remember: Promote a truth and it will grow; promote a fake and it will surely die. The rule is to promote that which can produce *results,* which are one of your best forms of self-promotion. In other words, you let your record speak for itself. Of course, if this is the best method, why should enlightened salespeople even worry about self-promotion? Shouldn't they just let the figures do all the talking? Indeed, a good record does speak for itself, but in today's competitive world there are many good records, and if you don't apply some self-promotion, you can get lost in the shuffle.

Of course, retailers have known this fact for years, promoting their own products. Take cola drinks, detergents, and coffee. The truth is most people cannot tell the difference between brands unless they look at the container. That's where image comes in and why companies spend millions promoting an image through advertising. Promotion is an indispensable tool to enhance the success of a product, and this fact is just as effective when applied to people.

Companies have no doubt about the necessity of promotion, but there is always debate about what type of promotion to concentrate their efforts on. Illustrating this is a story that's been floating around the advertising world for years. I guess it's true, but then again it might just be the business version of one of those traditional campfire stories, you know, like the babysitter who is plagued by threatening phone calls and the police say "Get out of the house, he's in the house." Anyway, this story is about a young Coca Cola marketing executive who goes into the president's office and boldly declares that he can save the company millions of dollars. According to his figures, they were spending way too much on advertising, at least 50 percent of which was ineffective. His idea was to slash the advertising budget by half, bringing it in line with his figures. Well, much to the young executive's surprise, the president immediately responded by saying, "I already know all that, but please, please, tell me which half we should cut and which half we should keep?"

Fortunately for our purposes, pinpointing where to concentrate our efforts in self-promotion will be much easier. In general, you will be successful in this area if you understand that **this endeavor is not just dependent on your ability, but also on your sociability.** Real self-promotion is a by-product of working through others, a result of winning the "people game."

WINNING THE PEOPLE GAME

When I was a little-leaguer, I thought the most important game you could play in was the World Series. Then, as sports seasons changed to basketball, football, and hockey, I focused my attention on their respective playoffs. It wasn't until I was much older that I realized these championships pale in comparison to the most important game you'll ever play: The People Game. If you win the people game you can have a great marriage, happy children, lifelong friends, and a satisfying career. So a lot is at stake.

How do you win the people game? The best place to start is by striving to understand human nature. In support of this contention, let me cite the Carnegie Institute, which after extensive research put forth this powerful observation: The main reason people fail is not because of a lack of talent or work, but a lack of understanding human nature. Along these lines, ponder the wisdom of Theodore Roosevelt, who wrote: "The single most important factor in being successful is being able to get along with people."

Self-promotion is a delicate combination of productivity and people ability. With this in mind, let's explore the principles needed to successfully win this biggest game of all.

Control the Middle

A study of the best strategies for winning at games and sports reveals the law: If you control the middle of the playing field, you can win the game! It's true; from passive games like chess to more vigorous contests like football, if you can dominate the middle, you can dominate the game. I believe the people game responds to the same strategy, however most people find it difficult to pinpoint exactly where the middle is.

The true middle in the people game is the other person's ego. The ego is the ultimate gate keeper. If you satisfy it, you can pass through and have a chance to get your ideas accepted and needs met. If you upset or put someone's ego on guard, however, they may prove to be a formidable opponent. Safe to say, most things are forgiven and forgotten except, perhaps, trampling on someone's ego. With this truth exposed, we must learn to understand this force to respect and direct it.

People Are Egocentric!   At our most basic level, the prime directive for everyone is to survive by obtaining pleasure and avoiding pain. It's the ego's job to see that these needs are met and it is relentless in this quest. As a result, everyone is egocentric. This isn't all bad, though; because besides immature egocentrics who try to satisfy their needs regardless of who they hurt, there are also mature egocentrics who realize that the most positive way to get their needs met is to first fulfill the needs of others, and that's good!

In addition to the survival instinct, the ego has other primary needs, which fall into three broad categories:

1. The need to garner **attention.**
2. The need to seek **assistance.**
3. The need to be **admired.**

In our quest for self-promotion, if we can satisfy these ego needs in others, we will prosper! Let's examine each ego need in greater detail.

STEP ONE—ATTENTION: *Never take anyone for granted.*

As egocentrics we all crave attention. Show business tells us we should be nice to everyone on the way up, because we'll see them again on the way down. Let's modify that statement for our purposes by saying: Be nice to everybody on the way up and they'll see to it that you stay there.

The wise salesperson will never underestimate the power and influence of the individual. From the janitor to the president, the savvy salesperson strives to treat everyone like somebody important. They know how many sales careers have been made and broken by the so-called "little people." These folks may not be in the spotlight, but they are still very much a part of the show.

Take, for instance, the secretary who schedules appointments for your largest client, or the folks in delivery, or that timid person in accounting. All of these people wield power and are part of your overall success. If you ignore them and become aloof, sooner or later you'll pay for it! Everybody wants to feel like a somebody, so treat them that way. If people get the impression they're being taken for granted, especially by someone puffed up with self-importance, it won't be long before they'll find a way to rudely bring that person back to reality. By the same token, if people feel you're interested in them, they'll go out of their way to help you.

So the process of promoting oneself begins with building a positive consensus of opinion, person by person. The best way to start this process is to try to communicate the unique value each person has whenever you come in contact with them. The first rule is: **If you want others to notice you, you must first notice others.**

In practice, intelligent salespeople will make a point to introduce themselves, not just to the "important people" but to everyone they may have dealings with, no matter how seemingly incidental. The wise salesperson will first make good eye contact, ask for the person's name, and inquire about feelings and duties. All of this is done with the goal of giving the person a sincere compliment or word of encouragement. It's amazing what a positive effect this can have on boosting one's career. Think of it as planting seeds, seeds of goodwill which will eventually grow to help you.

What's in a Name?   Dale Carnegie, the pioneer of human relationship studies, said, "A person's name is the most important sound heard in any language." A fundamental strategy to getting ahead in the people game is remembering the names of the people you meet. Nothing short of a cash gift impresses people more than being called by name. It doesn't matter what method you use — word association, notes, or repetition, just make the effort to remember people's names. A lot of people treat this point with a heavy dose of lip service. They think, I know all that, let's get on to the more complicated stuff. However, probably less than 5 percent of salespeople become proficient in remembering names, yet this is the first step in developing relationships, which are the key to self-promotion. Remembering names is a valuable skill that must be mastered.

STEP TWO — ASSISTANCE: *Look to serve others.*

As egocentrics, we are all looking for help to fulfill our plans and needs. One of the men I most admired, my wife's grandfather, died a couple of years ago. In thinking about what made him special, one quality stood out among many: He had a true desire to serve others. Although he wasn't a man of great distinction, he garnered the respect of everyone who knew him. No wealth, no power, no unusual achievements, yet at his funeral traffic was stopped on both sides of a four-lane highway to show respect for his passing. Everyone called him "Pa," and people loved him because he took such an interest in helping others. He was always the first to assist a neighbor who was trying to fix a car or put on a new roof. His home was always open and he always had a kind word for you, whether family or stranger, and a large helping of whatever was simmering on his stove.

I suppose we all know someone like Pa. These wonderful people are great examples of service in action. To be sure, this attitude should also be applied to our business. Although we don't necessarily have to fix cars or be a good cook, there are other ways to serve our business associates that are just as meaningful.

Serving others is visible proof that you care about them. You're backing up your words of recognition with action, which lends credibility to yourself, your product, and your company. Serving others is without question the fastest way of being noticed and recognized.

I once had the pleasure of working with a great salesperson who had mastered this concept. One day while I was casually telling some people in our office about a problem I was having with my golf swing, he was listening. To my surprise, on my desk the next morning was a golf magazine with an article promising to cure my problem. Attached to the magazine was a note that said, "Hope this will help. Your friend, Bob."

It was a little thing Bob did, but it endeared him to me. He became my friend, which, by the way, is no small thing. For as Mark McCormack, the wildly successful author and sports representative, pointed out, "All things being equal, people will do business with a friend. All things being unequal, people will still do business with a friend." Anyway, the golf lesson in the article didn't work, but the lesson Bob taught me about self-promotion did. It's precisely this type of gesture that makes a big difference in how people feel about you.

Of course, a lot of people in business think serving others means getting a client a good delivery date or checking on how they're doing from time to time. These actions are certainly good, but they're the norm and to be expected. The kind of service the extraordinary salesperson provides goes well beyond what's expected. Such salespeople not only fill the business needs of those around them, but are also aware of the personal needs of associates. I'm not suggesting that you suddenly become the corporate version of Mother Teresa! I'm simply saying that if you help people on a personal level, you will become an asset to them, and an asset is always noticed, promoted, and preserved.

Ultimately then, assisting and serving others is an easy task when, first and foremost, you find out what they are interested in and look for ways to help them fulfill that interest. When you find ways to serve others without reservation, you'll find people who will want to help and promote you in return.

STEP THREE—ADMIRATION: *Communicate and congratulate.*

As egocentrics, we long to be valued, appreciated, and admired and we will quickly form alliances with people who provide this. As we've seen, performance, attention, and assistance are proven steps to self-promotion. Completing the picture is a powerful practice which I call **communicate and congratulate.**

The prudent salesperson of today knows that the most noticed and appreciated people in life are those who encourage others to complete a task. In addition they are the first to congratulate others for a job well done. Business relationships must be nurtured by regular communication in order to survive. Failing to do this, especially in the area of self-promotion, is an opportunity missed. In today's competitive world, a missed opportunity is a luxury no one can afford. Communication is the very basis of human relationships, which are fundamental to self-promotion. The question that arises is, What form of communication should be utilized and what message should be conveyed? This communication vehicle must be unique and highly visible.

The Power of the Letter

You'll probably be surprised that the vehicle I feel does this best is the personalized letter. That's not to say visits, phone calls, and fax machines should be abandoned, just that, in my mind, the personalized letter delivers a significant impact and is the medium of choice of many of the most successful salespeople of today.

The written word has always been a highly valued form of communication in business. Possibly because it takes time and care to produce, and the written record endures long after the visit is over and the phones are quiet. Not to mention the fact that there's no better feeling than to receive a letter bearing good news! I feel that people who care to write and send letters are people who stand out in the crowd.

In reviewing the lives of many great men and women, it's apparent that most realized the value of the personal letter. For example, Theodore Roosevelt, adventurer, naturalist, soldier, politician, and statesman, left a legacy of hundreds of thousands of personal letters. It is said that at times Teddy wrote as many as fifty letters before 10 A.M. Another great practitioner of the letter and a hero of mine is the incomparable Margaret Thatcher. In her climb to becoming the first woman prime minister in European history, Lady Thatcher also became a master at using the personalized communiqué. Of course, regardless of the merits of the medium, the personal letter is only as good as the message it conveys.

The Message

What kind of message should the personalized letter contain in order to maximize our goal of self-promotion? Most pros feel the best theme is positive reinforcement. Truly nothing brightens your business day more than sincere words of encouragement and congratulations.

Of course, your clients and associates are already flooded with humdrum business correspondence like bills, sales advertisements, bills, and more bills, not to mention those wonderful corporate memos. So it is obvious that with a personal and positive approach your correspondence will be noticed as special and extraordinary.

Here are some examples of letters and messages that should give you a good idea of what I am talking about.

Dear Bill,
Thanks so much for choosing to do business with us.
It's a pleasure to be associated with someone with your insight and business skill.
Your friend,
Barry

Dear Sally,
I saw your sales figures for last month and I want to congratulate you on your performance. You're an inspiration to us all.
 Your friend and fellow worker,
 Barry

Dear Jeff,
It was good to see you last Thursday. It will be great to have you back at the office when your recovery is complete. We all miss you.
 Your friend,
 Barry

Dear Janet,
I wanted to acknowledge something that everybody should know. We have the best delivery department in the business. Thanks for going the extra mile.
 Sincerely,
 Barry

It's great to be on the receiving end of this type of letter. I think you can well imagine the uplifting effect this can have. The effects of these letters can be greatly enhanced by sending copies to upline managers and people important to the subject's career. This works wonders in compounding your letters' impact.

Of course, to some, this type of congratulatory communication may appear somewhat trivial, but **this is the little stuff that big dreams are made of.** Don't underestimate it.

If you agree that the personal letter is invaluable to promoting your career, here is a plan that will help you get started and be consistent: Each morning after arriving at your office, devote twenty minutes exclusively to letter writing. Do this before anything else. Whether you're a salesperson or sales manager, I encourage you to make this practice a priority, and you'll be surprised at the dividends it will reap.

Develop a Trademark

One of the unknown secrets to self-promotion is developing a trademark. The popular idea that salespeople
should be interested introverts, rather than interesting
extroverts, seems to make sense. However, that's not the
way things really work. I have found that customers like
dealing with characters, people who are professional yet
possess flair. This idea is fundamental to the main premise of this book, which is to be colorful yet always under
control. People with this balance are interesting and
attractive, and make for some powerful and exciting
interaction.

Strive to develop your own individuality, becoming as
interesting as reason permits. One way to do this is to
develop a trademark — something that sets you apart
from the crowd. A trademark can take many forms, from
the very subtle to the crass and obvious. To be on the safe
side, go with the subtle. It may be a nickname, personalized stationary, an unusual calling card, or simply a zeal-
ousness for quality. Whatever it is, it should distinguish
you from others. At its best, a trademark can create a
measure of notoriety for you while still maintaining a professional image. What should your trademark be? That's
something that you can discover for yourself, using the
following guidelines.

First, don't force it; make it fit your business. Also
don't make it too vainglorious; people don't like that.
Above all, be subtle and blend in with your team or
company's overall image. Avoid being a loose cannon.
Be it your Gucci briefcase, cowboy boots, or distinctive
ties, an appropriate trademark is an invaluable tool for
self-promotion.

Now to cap this pivotal chapter are some general guidelines vital to self-promotion. These we respectfully call
"The Ten Commandments of Dealing with People." I

know you'll find them useful in becoming a champion and winning the all-important people game.

THE TEN COMMANDMENTS OF DEALING WITH PEOPLE

1. **Avoid judging others.** Usually you only expose your your own faults.

2. **Don't give unasked-for advice.** People don't like it and neither do you.

3. **Adapt to the person you're with. Talk 1/3, listen 2/3.** Learn to communicate with the common and the extraordinary. If you listen, your popularity will soar.

4. **Don't gossip or betray secrets.** This leads others to mistrust you.

5. **Live and let live.** Quit trying to change people; you can barely change yourself.

6. **Admit when you're wrong.** Humility is always popular.

7. **Don't correct others on petty issues.** They don't like it and it's not not important.

8. **Act the way you want to be received.** Your attitude is echoed back to you.

9. **Settle conflicts person to person.** Not by committee. Go to the source first, without everyone knowing and taking sides.

10. **Be a cheerleader to others.** Never begrudge success of others. It costs nothing.

Finally, after it's all said and done, the mature salesperson knows that self-promotion isn't really about the self at all. Real self-promotion stems from satisfying others. The person who does the best job at this will naturally be promoted with the approval of all. So, with this information at hand we now have the tools to practice the art of self-promotion and winning the people game.

EXERCISES

A. In groups or individually, compose five short letters that successfully communicate and congratulate others.

B. Explore some possible trademarks you could utilize.

PART
2

THE TIMELESS FUNDAMENTALS OF SELLING

We are all salespeople every day of our lives, selling our ideas, plans, and enthusiasm to everyone we meet.
CHARLES M. SCHWAB

Chance favors the prepared mind.
LOUIS PASTEUR

5

APPOINTMENT BOOK:
A WINNER'S DIARY

Do not squander time, that's the stuff life's made of.
BENJAMIN FRANKLIN

We judge ourselves by what we think we can do, but others judge us by what we've done. Henry Wadsworth Longfellow wrote that while walking around Harvard 150 years ago. Keep it in mind, because accurately judging our performance is what this chapter is all about.

Probably like yourself, the first official action I took to prepare for selling was to purchase an appointment book. I quickly realized, however, that like pens and golf balls, you can't hope to own an appointment book; you just sort of lease one until it's lost or mistakenly borrowed. Then you lease another or, by chance, find one that's been floating around in the vast sea of missing-in-action business supplies.

When I lost my appointment book for the first time it was annoying, but certainly nothing to get too upset about. After all, an appointment book is just a reminder, right? See Mr. Smith at 9:00 A.M. — Meet so-and-so for lunch. Wrong! I found that the most important tool you will ever use in your sales career is your appointment book.

FACT: I know we are in an age of computer-assisted selling and gadgets of all types, but a survey of top executives would reveal that the appointment book is still king. In fact, whether paper or electronic, it's your best friend, a friend that will be brutally honest with you. An appointment book will act like a coach, who will applaud your strengths and expose your weaknesses. Of course having a weakness exposed is not pleasant, but it is something all champions bear. In so doing they become better, until they're the best, and this habit keeps them there.

During the sports season, coaches and players on pro and collegiate teams faithfully sit down after each game and analyze their performance. The main way they do this is by viewing their game films. Through video play-by-play, they study what they did right and what went wrong. A lot of salespeople go through a similar ritual, but instead of using film they use their appointment books to get vital input on their performance. They know that **a monitored performance is always a better performance.** As a manager, whenever salespeople told me they were having problems making sales, the first place I looked was in their appointment book. Ninety percent of the time the problem was there.

USING THE BOOK

First, unless electronic, use a pencil when writing in your book. Appointment cancellations can be frequent occurrences, and ink is too permanent to accommodate these changes. And an appointment book full of penned-in but canceled meetings makes it harder to obtain an accurate picture of what really happened in the past.

Next, schedule time at the end of each week for an appointment with yourself. Use this time to review what you did that week. Try to distinguish between "productive time" spent and the salesperson's age-old nemesis "put-off time."

One method that conscientious salespeople use to increase their productive time is to place three-by-five-inch index cards on their dashboard, their desk, and in their appointment book. On each of these cards is written this question: Is what I'm doing right now advancing my career and generating wealth? This is a highly visible reminder of the importance of always engaging in productive time.

What is productive time? It's any time spent increasing your overall cash flow and production. Put-off time, of course, is just the opposite — any time spent in activities that keep you from engaging in productive time. Your ability to engage in productive time and reduce the put-off time, however, will directly govern how much success you'll achieve during your career.

One of the most frequently quoted statistics in sales states that 80 percent of all sales are made by only 20 percent of the sales force. I know what the 20 percent of successful salespeople are doing, but what are the other 80 percent up to? I used to believe they were just goofing off — and some are — but I found that most of these 80 percent really are working. Unfortunately, they're working at all the wrong things. It goes something like this: They arrive at the office at 8:30 A.M. to drink some coffee and read the paper. At 9:00 A.M. it's off to a sales meeting. They get back at 10:00 A.M. to make a few phone calls at their desk and do some paperwork. They do everything from mileage reports and expense records to next month's sales projections. Oh, the lies.

Now it's 11:45 A.M. and time for lunch, so they go with some close associates to solve all of the company's problems in just an hour and fifteen minutes. At 1:00 P.M. it's back to the office to finish up those important papers and prepare for the high point of the day: a 2:00 appointment with a prospective customer. The only problem is that while they were at lunch, their 2:00 appointment called and canceled. So, now what?

They can't hang around the office anymore; that would be pushing it. So it's out the door and into the car to engage in one of the most popular of salespeoples' activities. I call it windshielding. Windshielding is when you get into your car and drive aimlessly all over. town trying to figure out something useful to do. That's why you see middle-aged men dressed in suits playing video games in Kiddie World at 2:30 in the afternoon. Usually all this is good for two hours of wasted time, and with that under their belt, they go back into the office and see how everyone else's day went. Pretty soon, it's 5:00 P.M. and time to go home. Finally, at 5:45, they walk through their front door exhausted, no doubt believing they worked hard all day. The truth is they have indeed been consumed by their work, but basically accomplished nothing. It's a sad scenario, especially at the end of the month when the sales figures are posted and the bonus checks are distributed. These people always find themselves at the bottom with no clue as to how they got there.

Fortunately, if you begin to monitor your activities on a weekly basis, the reasons for success or failure will become apparent and you can take action to keep your performance on track.

For purposes of helping you chart your weekly performance, we'll look at the two most important components of productive time: your sales presentations and your appointments made.

Sales Presentations

It is absolutely essential that you calculate the number of sales presentations you've made during the past week. For this figure to be meaningful, though, you need to know your sales ratio. **A sales ratio is the average number of presentations necessary to obtain a completed sale.** You should be able to get this figure from your company's sales and marketing departments. If this information is not available, you'll have to estimate it until you have monitored your appointment book long enough to figure it out.

If, for instance, it takes an average of four presentations to make one sale, your sales ratio is 4 to 1. If you need to make an average of two sales per week to earn your desired income, you know you'll have to give a minimum of eight presentations per week. If you want more money, you just increase the number of presentations you give on a weekly basis and over time, if your sales ratio is correct, the averages will work to your benefit, increasing your income.

Knowing your sales ratio and the number of sales presentations you made last week will reveal exactly why you are or are not successful, as well as how many appointments you'll need to make for the next week to stay on track. Without question your sales ratio is a very important factor to be aware of.

Appointments

Obviously, before a presentation is made and a sale closed, the very first thing you must do is get an appointment. The previous discussion of sales presentations demonstrated the importance of making appointments and that they should be set with design and purpose.

In addition to your sales ratio, you will also need to discover another essential indicator. **Your appointment ratio is the average number of appointments you need to ensure that one is kept and a full presentation is given.** Regrettably, the sales business isn't immune to Murphyism; just because you make an appointment doesn't mean it will be kept. Many a salesperson has seen a promising week sour because appointments were canceled for any variety of reasons. So with this uncertainty, how can you guarantee you'll get enough appointments every week? The answer is, again, by using the power of large numbers.

One field that can teach us about the power of large numbers is the insurance industry. They know that with increased numbers comes increased predictability. The insurance industry has learned that you can't predict whether one client will live or die, but if you take a thousand clients of the same age, you can determine with remarkable accuracy how many will make a claim and how many won't. You can't predict anything about one person, but you can predict almost everything about a group of people. It's the same principle when making appointments.

To eliminate uncertainty in business you, too, will have to increase your numbers. You'll have to make more appointments than is seemingly necessary, expecting only some of them to turn into sales presentations. To do this efficiently, you must discover your appointment ratio.

Now let's put all this information together and show how it works in a practical way. For instance, in one particular company it was known that out of sixteen appointments made, only eight presentations would eventually be given. So the appointment ratio is 2 to 1. The known sales ratio for this company is 4 to 1, that is, it takes four presentations on average to obtain one sale. So the eight presentations given should yield two sales. **Simply put, sixteen appointments equals four presentations equals two sales.** If the commission is approximately $1,000 per sale, this much activity in one week should earn $2,000.

Knowing these ratios allows you to review each week's activity to ensure that these averages have a chance to work. If the activity in your appointment book falls short, you know exactly how many more appointments you need to book for the next week to stay on course and reach your income goal.

Another benefit of knowing your sales and appointment ratios is that they give you an indication of how fundamentally strong or weak you are in selling. For instance, if your sales ratio is 6 to 1 yet your company's overall sales ratio is only 4 to 1, you know that you have room for improvement, probably in the area of giving your presentation and closing. With this revelation, appropriate action can be taken.

Two Hours to Greatness

I know a sales manager named David who is, in my opinion, the consummate winner. He is blessed with a wonderful family, good health, and a competitive spirit. He is also a great maker and saver of money. Naturally, I asked him his secret. David responded — like all good salespeople do — with a question. He said, "Could you discipline yourself for two hours a week if I showed you it would make you financially successful in sales?" My answer was everyone's answer. "Sure I could."

He then explained to me that years ago he discovered a system that helped make him successful, and it revolved around just two hours per week. He told me it was obvious from the start that the person with the most appointments always wins. But he also shared with me that at one time he became utterly frustrated at his inability to fill his schedule. After looking at the problem, he came up with some excellent observations and solutions.

David found the real problem in making appointments to be mostly related to timing! He discovered that if he started on Monday morning and tried to set appointments to fill up his week, he almost always failed.

Why? Because by the time Monday rolled around, prospects and clients were already too involved in their hectic week to give him any of their precious time. The result was they either rejected his bid to make an appointment or gave him an indefinite put-off. In other words, he was a day late and dollars short.

Initially, he thought the solution was to make his appointments in advance. But he found that if appointments were made too far in advance, they were usually canceled or forgotten. So the trick became to find a time that would not be too far in advance to intimidate prospects yet soon enough to keep the appointments memorable. The solution, he discovered, was to spend an average of two hours, on Thursday or Friday, setting up appointments for the following week. Now no matter how busy Thursday or Friday became, the major objective of at least one of these days was to spend a total of two hours setting up new appointments for the next week.

It's basic common sense, yet most salespeople show up Monday morning with only a small percentage of their week booked. It then becomes a matter of chance whether their week will be a success or not. They could easily have saved themselves from this uncertainty if they preplanned their activity the week before.

There's another reason why the end of the week is the best time to book appointments. You know Monday and Friday are both workdays, but they are worlds apart in the attitudes they foster. I'm sure this feeling is universal. On Monday, we're all keyed-up, thinking about what we must accomplish and how we can get it done. On Friday, though, it's different; we're still working hard, but we can't help but think about the weekend. We feel good and less stressed. For this reason, when the phone rings on Friday and someone wants to make an appointment way off in the future, say, Wednesday, it seems easier to say yes, much more so than it would be on Monday morning.

The salesperson who makes appointments this way will have better timing and, come Monday, won't be caught flat-footed with nowhere to go! This system really works, and all the discipline it requires is two hours at the end of the week to set your appointments. Once the appointments are made, it's a simple task to see that they're kept.

Double-Booking

As stated, the only way to guarantee success in selling is by increasing your numbers. So you can really stack the odds in your favor by practicing a technique known as double-booking. For example, if you find that your particular line of selling is prone to high instances of cancellations, consider double- or even triple-booking by scheduling two or more appointments at the same time. That way if one cancels, you will still have backup appointments in reserve to fill the gap. What happens, you may ask, if none of the extra appointments cancel? This luxury allows you to keep the ones you feel are the most urgent or promising, and simply call the others explaining that due to business being so good, would they be gracious enough to allow you to reschedule? You'll probably be surprised at how accommodating clients will be. Rather than begging for appointments you'll be working from a position of strength. At any rate, you'll be maximizing your most valuable asset—time!

Here's another tip I got from a successful vice president of sales for a worldwide manufacturing company. This gentleman told me he never makes appointments on the hour. For example, when he and a client set an appointment for, say, 2:00, he would always ask if he could move the appointment to 2:15 to better accommodate his schedule. This always gave the correct impression that he was a busy salesperson and his time was at a premium.

HOW TO MAKE APPOINTMENTS

FACT: *You can become wealthy if you can master making appointments.*

Now that we know how to use our appointment books more effectively, the next step is to make an actual appointment. Whether you're the CEO or a wide-eyed rookie, the following is bedrock material for successful appointment making.

Be Prepared

Whether you use the phone or you're face-to-face, the real secret to making appointments is preparation. You must know exactly what to say at all times during the appointment-making process. To do this you should develop a phone or appointment script and then memorize it using a tape recorder. Doing this builds confidence, and confidence will boost your overall performance. As Notre Dame's coach, Lou Holtz, pointed out, there is only one way to handle pressure and that's practice.

Match Communication Styles

While using the telephone for appointment making, many "greats" like to see themselves in a mirror. They feel this improves the quality of their voice. In addition to this, they also try to match the communication style of the prospect. For instance, if you detect that the prospect is a New Yorker and speaks at a fast pace, try to quicken your own tempo. Likewise, if a prospect speaks slowly and more deliberately, imitate this within reason. Of course, if you're face-to-face you'll not only want to match speaking styles but also body language. Doing this will put the prospect at ease and put you both on the same wave length. Please keep in mind, though, the trick is to imitate but not get caught doing it!

Reject Rejection

No discussion of appointment making would be complete without including humankind's age-old nemesis, rejection. In my mind, good salespeople are among the most courageous individuals on earth. Why? Because they confront and defeat rejection daily. Let's face it, rejection is painful and no matter how long you're in sales, you never really get used to it. Rejection hurts, and many people develop a fear of it to the point that it limits their success. The good news is, most winners want to win so badly that they learn to endure and tame rejection. The extraordinary salesperson beats rejection by keeping their eye on the goal, not the process. The trick is to depersonalize rejection by looking for pleasing results, not painless methods.

To forge past rejection when making appointments, always have a special goal in mind before you start. If it's six new appointments, don't give up until this goal is reached, whether it takes ten minutes or an hour. This way you'll end each session successfully, and any pain endured will seem worth it. Also consider rewarding yourself everytime you're rejected. Pay yourself five dollars, or work a deal with your spouse that a certain number of rejections entitles you both to an evening of romance. So until they develop a Teflon suit to protect against rejection, your best defense is to focus on the goal, depersonalize rejection, and turn it into something positive. In selling, you never know who will buy; those who should often don't and those you thought wouldn't, do! You can't prejudge; just make all the calls and handle any rejection philosophically.

Have One Objective

Your only objective when making an appointment is to make an appointment. So by all means, resist the temptation to give your presentation over the phone or in an inappropriate place. **Always sell the appointment, not the presentation.** Granted, sometimes this is difficult, especially when a prospect asks you those nasty questions like "What's this all about?" and "What are you selling?" To make an appointment, you should follow the reformed KISS technique: Keep it simple, and successful.

Big-Benefit Introduction

Start your appointment script by saying the prospect's name and introducing yourself, and then give a big-benefit reason why you should meet. After this, immediately close for the appointment. Unless you're using a referral or asking a question, it's best not to pause, keeping the process as brief as possible. The rule is the longer you talk, the less chance you have to succeed.

Casually Close by Choice

When you do close for the appointment, casually give the prospect a choice of possible times that you can meet, but be subtle and not too pushy.

"Mr. Prospect, I've set aside some time Tuesday morning for you, [pause], or would Wednesday after lunch be better?"

Whatever day they pick is fine, and now you suggest a specific time or let them choose if your schedule's flexible. By placing a decision about time before the prospect, you help to completely bypass the usual issue, which is, should the prospect grant you an appointment at all? The human brain can entertain only one thought at a time, so by making the prospect address the decision of time, you change the emphasis from if to when. This alternative-choice technique is a must for efficient appointment making. Just remember, be casual.

Be a Name-Dropper

When making appointments, use the influence of others as much as possible. This idea comes from the philosophy that if the seller tells something to the prospective buyer, the buyer may not perceive it as the truth. This is because the buyer thinks the salesperson has something to gain. However, if it can be shown that others who have nothing to gain have said the same thing, this will likely be perceived as the truth. A simple rule to keep in mind is, What I say is never as convincing as what others say. Use brief testimonials from satisfied customers wherever possible. This also works for service-selling older accounts, where name-dropping and spreading news of satisfied customers keeps regular accounts sold. Of course, the use of referrals is so vital that we devote all of Chapter 10 to it.

Objectives and Put-offs

No matter what you attempt to do in life, the seeds of opposition have already been sown. So when you attempt to make an appointment, you'll often be faced with obstacles. One of these is the put-off. This is where a prospect doesn't have the courage to outright say no to an appointment. Instead, they will try to stall and keep the appointment from ever happening. The best tactic to employ to deal with the put-off is polite persistence and regular communication. Unlike the extraordinary salesperson, most give up on prospects way too soon. The reason for this behavior is lack of organization and backbone. Figures show that the average salesperson calls a prospect only twice, and if nothing transpires, they let this prospect fade into obscurity. It's only when these salespeople are cleaning out their cars about a year later, that they discover the prospect's old business card under the floormat. Then they realize they should have followed-up better, but since so much time has gone by, they're too embarrassed to call back.

To avoid this, keep a log of all your prospects. Some salespeople use their computers for this, utilizing some of the great sales software available. At present, I still prefer to use a thirty-day and a twelve-month card-file system. If I call on a prospect on the first of the month and need to call again in two weeks, I note this on a three-by-five card which I place in the thirty-day file marked for the fourteenth of the month. Then on the morning of the fourteenth, I check my box and, presto, instant memory recall. The twelve-month card file works the same, with one card denoting each month. Remember, never drop a prospect unless they die or give you an emphatic NO. This way you will develop a systematic approach that will yield more appointments.

The best salespeople know that it may take five, six, or even more tries to successfully secure an appointment. Never give up too early! But what can you do to help reduce the need for constant callbacks? Here's a great technique: **Never give someone the chance to say no to you twice in any ten-second period.** Using this strategy, whenever you encounter a put-off first politely seek to find common ground and then try again. Here's how it works:

Suppose you ask a prospect for an appointment by casually giving a choice of times ("Thursday morning or maybe Friday?"). The prospect responds with "Sorry, I'll be in Denver on business." Rather then saying "What about next week?" which gives the client the chance to put you off by saying, "Call me back later," here is a better way to respond:

Salesperson:	Denver, that's a great town. Do you get to go there often?
Client:	Sometimes.
Salesperson:	What do you like best about the city, or do you like it?
Client:	Well, yes, it's a beautiful location, plus it's a clean and prosperous town.
Salesperson:	I know you'll have a great trip. When will you be back?
Client:	Oh, I'm just going for four days.
Salesperson:	Say, let's make our appointment for either Wednesday about 11:15, or would Thursday at 10:00 be better?
Client:	I'm sorry, I'll be golfing; that's my day off. And Thursday I'm all booked up.
Salesperson:	Golfing, I love golf. Where do you play?
Client:	I play at Snob Valley Country Club.
Salesperson:	Snob Valley, that's a tough course. What's your handicap?
Client:	Eight.
Salesperson:	Good for you, we'll have to play sometime. Now I understand why Wednesday is out of the question, but let's see . . . , how about the Monday after that at 9:00, or would later Tuesday be better?
Client:	Well, let's see. I guess that Monday would be all right.
Salesperson:	Great. How's early morning?
Client:	8 A.M. is good for me.
Salesperson:	Great, I'll see you then and I'll be interested on how your trip and golf game went. Take care.

By seeking some common ground you keep the prospect talking. This acts as a critical cooling-off period, allowing you to reset the appointment without appearing like you're badgering the prospect. Of course, normally you want to keep the appointment-making process short and sweet. When you're faced with put-offs, however, your strategy must change. When this happens, your main objective is to keep the prospect talking long enough to overcome the put-off. The same strategy applies to encountering objections, which are the subject of Chapter 8. In all fairness, the following section reveals two powerful objection killers for helping to secure appointments.

Deflections and Reverses

Deflections and reverses will help handle the classic objections we often hear, like, "I'm not interested," "No thanks" and "Drop dead!" Let's use the deflection first.

Salesperson: Hello, Mr. Jones, my name is so-and-so with ABC Corporation. I'm calling, Mr. Jones, because our company has some fresh ideas on inventory control that is really shaking up the industry.

Prospect: Look, thanks but no thanks, I'm just not interested.

Salesperson: Mr. Jones, this may sound funny but I'm kind of glad you said that. You see, that's what many of our best customers said before they got to know us. Anyway, regardless of your buying position, I just want to at least get acquainted. Would Monday morning be acceptable? Or might Wednesday be a better option for a very short meeting?

The **"I'm not interested"** objection stops a lot of salespeople cold because they badger the client or counter with tired old lines like "You mean to tell me you're not interested in making money?" The deflection works a lot better because it gracefully sidesteps the objection and keeps on going. It's not foolproof, but it at least gives you a fighting chance to make an appointment. To deflect, just agree with the prospect and tell them all your best customers say that. Then continue toward your objective. This will be to secure an appointment or gain more information.

Now let's demonstrate a classic reverse, used against the "I'm not interested" objection:

"Mr. Jones, don't worry about it, that's perfectly all right, but for future reference may I ask why you're not too enthused about inventory control at this time?"

The reverse works by taking the statement of the prospect and sending it back to them in question form. The idea is to keep the prospect talking until a need might be exposed.

Final Resistance Breaker

If after using these methods the prospect stands firm in their "I'm not interested" pose, don't give up! Try the following appointment savers.

The Three Promises This technique is a lifesaver and has made Yours Truly many appointments that seemed hopelessly lost.

Prospect: Look, Barry, I'm busy and really not interested.

Salesperson: Okay, Mr. Jones, I understand, but let me make you three promises.

1. If you're not interested after we've met five minutes, I'll leave and you'll never see me again.

2. I won't try to do any business with you the first time we talk.

3. I'll promise to forget about selling and concentrate only on seeing if I can honestly be of service to you again. If I can't, I'll tell you and go.

Mr. Jones, I know there's a real chance that I won't be able to help you, but I would at least like to meet you and acquaint you with our company. Would Monday or Wednesday be better?

Information Lure   If you still get a no response and the prospect is losing patience, try this option using the line of information:

Salesperson: Mr. Jones, even if you're not interested, you still qualify for some free information that many of your industry associates have found invaluable. Would you like a free packet for your files?
Prospect: Yes.
Salesperson: Fine, Mr. Jones, I'll drop it off next time I'm in your area. Now, I would like to at least meet you when I deliver it. Would Monday morning . . .

If you are fortunate enough to be able to travel to your prospects, this technique can really pay off. Many times when you deliver the information, the prospect will soften and grant your appointment. By the way, if they tell you to just mail the material, hesitate, within reason, and insist that you need to guarantee hand-delivery.

With all this in our arsenal, let's continue with an example of an appointment, using some of the techniques presented in this chapter as well as a few other key phrases that you may find useful.

Salesperson: Mr. Smith, my name is Barry Munro. I know we have never met but we do have a mutual acquaintance, Mr. Dan Jones from XYZ Company. You do know Dan, don't you?

Client: Yes, I do.

Salesperson: Well, Mr. Smith, I did some work for Dan and XYZ, and Dan was really excited with the results and suggested I give you a call. I'd like to meet you and briefly share what Dan is so excited about. Would around 3:00 Monday be feasible, or would Tuesday be better for you?

Client: OK, what are you selling?

Salesperson: Mr. Smith, I've heard it said that everyone is selling something, and if I had to put a label on it I guess I'm sharing an idea. An idea many of your peers in business have found makes a lot of sense. But you'll have to decide that for yourself. Right?

Client: Right, but what's it all about?

Salesperson: Well, Mr. Smith, if I could give you the information you needed over the phone and get the information I needed, I would do it and it would save me a lot of time, but I can't. It can't be done over the phone, so let me suggest we meet for a short time and discuss the possibilities that may or may not exist between us. So, would Monday at 3:00 be good or is Tuesday a better choice?

Client: No, that wouldn't be good. I'm booked up Monday and Tuesday. I have to speak to our stockholders.

Salesperson: That's great, Mr. Smith, do you enjoy speaking?

Client: Yes, I do now.

Salesperson: I know speaking is a real art, but I guess the more you do it the more comfortable you become.

Client: That's true.

Salesperson: Well, I hope your speech goes well. Anyway,
                 instead of those days let's make it Friday
                 and you pick the time.
Client: Let's see, I guess Friday at 1:15 will work.
Salesperson: Great, Mr. Smith, I'll see you then.

Like everything in life, the more you do something, the
better at it you become. So when you're first making
appointments, don't expect things to go perfectly, just
persevere and keep making appointments. Remember:
**You have to be bad before you can be good and you have
to be good before you can be great.** Becoming great at
something is inevitable if you keep trying.

Time Is Money Approach

Here's an add-on technique that's been used very successfully on certain types of prospects, especially home-
owners, hourly-wage earners, and small business people.
This technique is appropriate for a prospect who is
extraresistent in giving an appointment.

Salesperson: So would Monday, say, after dinner be good
                 or is Thursday better for you?
Client: No, I don't think so. I am really busy. Why
                 don't you call me back in a couple of
                 months and I'll talk to you then.
Salesperson: Well, I can certainly understand your being
                 busy and, besides, it may cost you money to
                 take valuable time discussing an idea that
                 may or may not be beneficial, right?
Client: That's right.
Salesperson: Mr. Prospect, I hope I'm not prying, but
                 can you tell me approximately how much
                 you think a half hour of your time is worth?

Client:	Well, that's easy. I make twenty dollars an hour, so, I guess about ten dollars.
Salesperson:	That's good. I'll tell you what, your time is valuable, so here's what I'll do. Let's go ahead and meet anyway for about fifteen minutes. At the end of this time if you feel I haven't shared anything of value with you, I'll write you a check for a full half hour for your time and be on my way. Fair enough? Now would Monday or Thursday be better?
Client:	OK, let's try Monday.
Salesperson:	Great, I'll see you at 6:00. Oh! Can we move that back to 6:15?
Client:	OK, see you then.

Naturally, to use this technique you will have to be confident in the fact that the profits from any sale will be worth the possible cost of a few appointments. Please note, you'll seldom actually have to pay for an appointment, however; it seems the whole exercise just shows the prospect your sincerity.

Hunting Big Game

It's a lot easier to hunt jackrabbits than it is elephants. Likewise, it's less problematic to make small sales than it is the million-dollar ones. For the big accounts, your highest hurdle is often just getting with the right person. The big hitters are usually well protected and extremely busy. To penetrate you have to consider some creative prospecting. Early breakfasts, golf tournaments, eye-popping facsimiles, invitations to special after-convention parties, and my favorite strategy which, for lack of a better name, I call **Orders from Headquarters.** Here's how it works. If I'm calling a big account in Los Angeles, I'll first call their corporate headquarters in, say, New York. I try to talk to the highest-level representative in the division I'm selling. Even though they can't help me, I get the biggest name in the department and through their assistance, I get a referral or the contact whom I should be seeing in L.A. Then I simply call the Los Angeles branch, ask for this individual by name, telling them in truth that the home office suggested that I call. This simple strategy gives my call a more favorable reception, often resulting in an appointment.

Confirming Appointments

Never make the novice mistake of confirming an appointment over the phone. This just invites cancellations by the score. I never confirm local appointments. If I must travel a distance, however, I will confirm but only by using a short personalized letter. Appointments are too valuable to throw away by catching someone at a bad time while making a telephone confirmation.

In conclusion, the best salespeople are masters at making appointments and they monitor their performance using their appointment book. This practice shows them where they've been and where they're going. It also lets them know the real reason why they are or are not successful. Finally, the great salespeople understand the value of knowing their sales and appointment ratios. They will always have enough deliberately planned that nothing is left to chance, especially their success.

EXERCISES

A. Conduct a time study to document how effectively your time is being spent.

B. In groups or individually, compose your own appointment-making scripts, memorizing them word for word utilizing video and audio to assist in the learning process.

C. Examine the strength of your purpose because **it is your purpose itself that will supply the initiative to making more appointments.**

6

THE PRESENTATION

*There's nothing more powerful than
an idea whose time has come.*
VICTOR HUGO

Perhaps you've never considered this, but the real difference between golf and bowling becomes apparent only
when you drop the ball on your foot. Fortunately, when
you're talking about the differences found in the sales
world, there is no need for such painful demonstrations.
For instance, take the differences between the amateur
and the pro in sales. Here, there are many points of contrast, but perhaps the most striking are in the quality of
the presentations they give. Unlike the amateur, the pros
all have the ability to give a great sales presentation. What
does the extraordinary salesperson's presentation contain
that others' don't? How can we make our presentations
meet these same high standards? This chapter explores
the fundamental elements of great sales presentations:
structure, adaptability, sincerity, evidence, entice and
withdraw, empathy, focus, and the use of questions and
humor. But first, along with these fundamentals, let's

DOERS

• Pushy Hard Closers   A   • Sales Achievers

POOR — C – o – m – m – u – n – i – c – a – t – i – o – n — GOOD

• Order Takers   o   • Socializers

WATCHERS

FIGURE 6.1   The Four Main Types of Salespeople

look closer at the people doing the presenting, because regardless of the quality and format of the message, it's only as good as the messenger.

To be sure, most messengers — or should I say salespeople — want to do well; they have good intentions. The age-old problem is that customers have to perceive these good intentions. The salespeople who are perceived best seem to excel in two areas: communication and action. These two areas of measurement are denoted in Figure 6.1.

The first area of measurement is displayed by a horizontal line spelling out the word **communication.** To the extreme left of the line are the poor communicators, to the extreme right, the good. Good communicators are salespeople who can convey ideas while still listening and responding to the thoughts of others. They are perceived as caring, enthusiastic, and (very important) likeable. The poor communicator is just the opposite, having a more monotonous approach and being viewed as cold, having little regard for the wants of those they are talking to.

The second area of measurement is represented by a vertical line spelling out the word **action.** At the top of the line are the energetic doers, who take action and make things happen. At the bottom are the more passive watchers, who take action only when necessary. The horizontal word **communication** and vertical word **action** intersect in the figure. At each corner of this cross is found a distinct category of salesperson.

THE FOUR MAIN TYPES OF SALESPEOPLE

Pushy Hard Closers

These are aggressive people of action, but they do not possess good communication skills. This causes them to be seen by the customer as cold, opinionated, pushy, and self-serving — the classic hard closer. They are sometimes abusive to customers, and the public disdains them. Surprisingly, they see themselves as energetic go-getters who are doing a great job.

Socializers

The opposite of the pushy hard closer is the socializer. This type of salesperson is low on initiative but possesses good communication skills. With these qualities, the socializer mainly sells by building friendships. They love to talk and are usually good for a joke or two. The problem is they rely too much on friendship and not enough on their performance. This causes them to be perceived by customers as nice people, but somewhat ineffective in solving problems. Friendship is an integral part of selling, but you also want clients to buy because they respect you and your product's ability to perform.

Order Takers

Some companies and salespeople find themselves in the enviable position of being the only game in town. Because of this, customers have no choice but to deal with them. This climate is often the realm of our third group of salespeople, the order takers. They are low on energy and action and are also very poor communicators. This unhealthy combination causes them to be perceived by customers as inept, lethargic, boring, and cold. Not surprisingly, as soon as the competition appears and customers have a choice, the order taker is the first casualty. With their lack of skills, they just can't compete.

Sales Achievers

Finally we come to the most optimum group of salespeople, the sales achievers. These people possess excellent communication skills and have the initiative and energy to make things happen. With these balanced qualities, sales achievers tactfully uncover the needs and desires of customers, then they follow through with action to satisfy them. There is little difference between the intentions of the sales achiever and the customer's perception of those intentions. Sales achievers are enthusiastic, hardworking, and well liked for their social skills. They are also respected for their technical prowess. Truly this is the group we should all strive to be a part of. This balance of action and good communication skills should be our guiding influence when we apply the following information outlining the elements of a great presentation.

ELEMENTS OF A GREAT SALES PRESENTATION

Structure

To develop consistency and quality, a presentation must have structure; you can't just ad lib your way to the top.

The entire sales process breaks down into three distinct phases.

1. The **Investigative Phase** involves prospecting, appointment making, contact, and qualifying.
2. The **Informative Phase** involves showing in detail what your product or service does. This is the presentation phase.
3. The **Impact Phase** is the close, referrals, and service.

To lead into your presentation, you should have already performed three essential duties — set a sales goal, make contact, and qualify.

Set a Sales Goal This is a much-overlooked step in the selling process. But unless you have a specific goal in mind, your best efforts can lack concentration and results. To set a sales goal you will be influenced by many factors. For instance, the size of the account, financial capacity, past buying patterns, and special incentives the company is offering. This research can be enhanced by keeping detailed notes on what transpired on previous sales calls. A sales goal makes every sales call more meaningful.

Contact and Qualifying When you first meet your prospect it's important to do all the standard things well. You know: firm handshake, no palm tickling, good eye contact, smile, and proper dress. The rule for attire is quality not quantity, and you should dress like the people your client already trusts — like their banker, their business associates, the CEO of their company. With these preliminaries taken care of, you can focus on the primary function of initial contact, which is to relax and get to know the prospect. This is client bonding (but unlike male bonding, you won't have to employ primal screaming). All you need to do is get the client talking about themselves as much as possible; while this is occurring, you seek areas of agreement.

Try to spend no more than five minutes talking about family, background, sports, or common acquaintances. You can use the F.O.R.M. method as a conversation guide: *family* first; *occupation* or business background second; *recreation,* sports and hobbies third; and your *message,* which in this case will come later. From here begin qualifying by asking general questions about their business.

Your goals in qualifying are:

1. Determine needs.
2. Access client's financial capacity.
3. Make sure you're speaking to the real buyer.

As stated, this information will be acquired by listening and questioning. For instance, during the qualifying you may ask, "Mr. Prospect, who, along with yourself, would be responsible for any final buying decision?" This would let you know if you're talking to the right person. For budget and special needs, you'll have to develop subtle questions pertinent to their industry, which will allow you to approximate their financial strength. Qualifying not only gives you the green light to go ahead, it also shows you the direction.

The Big Question   After the preliminary questions, you should ask a question that really cuts to the chase. For instance,

Salesperson:	Mrs. Green, overall, what would you say it would take for you to want to do business with our firm?
or	Mr. Jones, off the record, under what circumstances would you give serious consideration to using us as a supplier?
or a more subtle approach	Mrs. Green, I know this sounds a little unusual, but what would you say is your most important goal in business and in life?

Often open-ended probes like this can save time and possible gridlock by getting right to the point. These questions often surprise customers with their honesty and directness, and the answers customers give go right to the heart of their needs. Using a big question such as one of these helps to really kick-start your presentation.

Adaptability—The A Curve

The world is full of paradoxes, some profound like: To be a great leader, you must be a great follower! Some less profound like: To make a golf ball fly high, you must hit it sharply down. (In this latter pursuit, I am the distinguished holder of the world record for the largest divot ever taken. It weighed just under twenty pounds, advanced my ball two feet, and nearly broke both my arms.) Anyway, there is also a fundamental paradox in giving your presentation: On one side you need a very structured presentation, but you also have to be adaptable and ready to change. This is because you're dealing with the different moods of people and you can't treat them all the same during your presentation.

THE A CURVE
Prospect's Initial Response at Contact

```
                                          ALLIANCE
                    +                        /
                                         ACCURATE
                                           /
                                       AMIABLE
                                        /
                              ACADEMIC
                                  /
              —              ADVERSARIAL
                                  ⁻
                        ADECISIVE ⁻
    APATHETIC ————————
```

The preceding diagram shows why you'll need to flavor your presentation according to the different moods that prospects can display. These moods are nothing new, and salespeople have been developing different strategies to offset them for years. (In fact, I recall my father giving me advice on handling apathetic and adversarial prospects years ago using the take-away technique.) The bottom of the curve represents your hardest challenge when presenting a product or service. As you move up the curve you're dealing with clients whose moods and character are still challenging, yet more conducive to selling. Your objective is to accommodate a prospect and bring them up the curve to where they can take an unbiased look at what you're offering. This is the neutral position denoted by the word accurate near the top of the curve.

As a practical example, suppose you were selling to an apathetic client. Your task would be create interest, bringing the prospect up the curve to the point where they'll take an accurate look at your proposal. After reaching this accurate stage, ideally you can both move to the top of the curve and form an *alliance,* resulting in a sale. Each mood or type of prospect depicted on the curve should be handled a little differently. That's why you need to be adaptable.

The Apathetic   The apathetic prospect doesn't believe you can make a difference. You've got to show them you can and shock them into giving a response, hot or cold. They must be encouraged to participate throughout the presentation. The apathetic person's wood is wet, and you've got to dry it off to start a fire.

Perhaps the best strategy to use on the apathetic prospect is to show them what you have but give them the impression they can't have it. This is known as "the entice and withdraw" or "take-away technique," which is discussed in detail later in this chapter.

The Adecisive   The adecisive prospect is a real gem.
They can barely make up their mind whether or not to
take the next breath. The adecisive is looking for a leader
to take charge. With this type you have to take command
and be bolder than normal, telling them what they need,
why they need it, and how much they're gonna buy. With
adecisive prospects, you have to decide. This can work
only if you put the client first and don't take advantage of
their weakness. Sell them what they really need!

The Adversarial   This is my favorite type of prospect.
They're full of you-know-what and vinegar and put on a
good front that they don't like you or your company.
They'll contradict you and fuss all the way through your
presentation. But if you treat them nicely, challenge them
with a little humor, and show you're not afraid of them,
over time they can become your best customers — giving
everybody else hell but staying true to you.

The Academic   To be in an academic mood is to be cautious: just the facts and lots of them, please. Perhaps this
prospect's job is on the line or they've been burned by
other salespeople. A person in this mood must be treated
like the detail personality type, using E2L2 (see Chapter 3).
This means twice the logic and lots of proof, testimonials,
and guarantees.

The Amiable   The last mood type is the amiable prospect.
A prospect like this may sometimes be overly agreeable;
they may even insist that they don't need a presentation
and are ready to sign up. As tempting as this may be, you
should insist on giving a presentation. If you don't, misunderstanding can occur down the road, at which point
the amiable prospect forgets that they turned down a presentation and feels you purposely misled them. Without a
presentation, an amiable's mood can quickly turn hostile.

Though a great sales presentation must have structure and routine, the extraordinary salesperson must be flexible to all the changing situations that may arise, as represented by the A curve diagram.

Sincerity

George Burns once said that the key is sincerity, and if you can fake that, you've got it made. However, to be insincere is a little like trying to cover up the taste of cod liver oil: No matter what you put in it, the taste will always come through. It's the same in a presentation: You can't mask insincerity. If you're insincere, it will always show through, and nothing is more destructive to your presentation.

To develop sincerity, you first must possess a deep-rooted, heartfelt belief that what you're doing is meaningful and noble. I think this quote by advertising great Bruce Barton sums it up nicely: "The essential element in personal magnetism is a consuming sincerity and an overwhelming faith in the importance of the work one has to do." There's perhaps nothing more shallow than a salesperson whose only motivation is the money they'll make. To develop sincerity, you must first identify the benefit your product offers to others. You can then make this benefit the focal point of all your selling and, as a by-product, a financial reward will be received. Remember this formula:

Benefit = belief = sincerity = success = money

Reversing this equation by putting all your emphasis on financial reward will seldom produce the sincerity needed to yield long-term success. It's important not to trivialize this point. To prove it, answer the following question.

QUESTION: *Would you rather fight a war with patriots or mercenaries on your side?*

If you answered patriots, you'd be wise. Based on historical record, the patriot is much more likely to win a fight than the mercenary, because monetary motivation is simply not enough to sustain an effort over time. When the going really gets tough, you've got to have a cause that, when fought for and won, justifies your existence, giving you a clear conscience along with a full stomach. A lot of people's only goal is to make the big bucks. These profiteers seem to always be hopping from one thing to another, looking for the big payoff, which seldom shows up. Sadly, these folks fail to understand that it's the *crusader,* who has found a purpose to strongly believe in that ends up with the most success and satisfaction. Belief and sincerity give you the endurance to win.

Sincerity can come only from purpose and the belief that what you are doing is right. Now, do you really believe there is a benefit to your customers in what you're selling? If you don't, you will lack the cornerstone upon which all great presentations are built. Remember, you can't fool anybody, including yourself, so find something to believe in, and sincerity will be a guaranteed byproduct.

A Body of Evidence

With each presentation you should plan to show at least two bodies of evidence supporting the key concepts you wish to propose. To accomplish this, use E2L1 with some additions:

- Use emotional opening to create interest.
- Provide facts or logic.
- Substantiate facts with evidence, reports, testimonials, brochures, or test results.
- Use emotional ending showing the benefit to customer.

Using the above formula try to have modular bodies of
evidence ready for each customer's possible hot buttons,
such as service, quality, cost saving, and so on.

By labeling and filing each self-contained body of evidence, you won't be caught fumbling for paperwork
when a client asks questions or expresses a need.

Entice and Withdraw

Sometimes in order to make a deal, you've got to be
ready to blow a deal. I've never met a great salesperson
who at some point in the sale didn't give this impression
by using "entice and withdraw." This is done with the
belief that most people want what they can't have and
something becomes more valuable when there's a chance
you could lose it. It's very much like the situation found
in young relationships, the teenager who takes a steady
date for granted until that date expresses an interest in
someone else. Suddenly the desirability of the steady date
increases dramatically.

Perhaps an even better example of entice and with-
drawal is found in the art of fishing. Here, when bait is
presented to fish, they oftentimes pay little attention to it.
However, if the bait is quickly withdrawn, an aggressive
fish will often change character and vigorously chase the
bait, striking at it decisively. That's the positive effect of
entice and withdraw.

Likewise in selling, customers will often display this
same type of apathy. And unless you practice a little
entice and withdraw, you'll go home with no catch. But
how does entice and withdraw work in sales? Following
are a few examples that should help you get the idea.

EXAMPLE ONE: *The False Start Technique.*

Salesperson: (Entice) And as you can see, Mr. Jones, this
                  product saved one of our clients 35 percent

on their bottom line. They loved it.
(Withdraw) [Smile] But Mr. Jones, as busy as
you are, I'm not sure you have the time to
listen to this great idea.

Client: No, no, go ahead.

EXAMPLE TWO: *(Spoken very low-key.)*

Salesperson: *(Entice)* This is our top-of-the-line model and
it's a favorite of our biggest customers.
(Withdraw) But you'd probably like to see
something else.

Client: Well, not necessarily. You see we're growing
. . . so go ahead, show me what your other
customers bought.

EXAMPLE THREE: *This one helps on the close, especially for
insurance, service contracts, and credit accounts.*

Salesperson: *(Entice)* Well, I think you made an excellent
choice.
(Withdraw) Now all we have to do is see if
you can qualify.

Client: What do you mean qualify? Is there a problem?

Salesperson: No, it shouldn't be for you, but let's get
some information down on paper just to
make sure. Fair enough?

By practicing entice and withdraw during your presentation, you introduce an element of danger, which will
increase your client's anxiety. This will make your product or service more desirable and easier to sell. At least
one time during your presentation, practice the art of
entice and withdraw by briefly and subtly taking away
from your client the opportunity to buy.

Empathy

Empathy is the ability to understand and be sensitive to what other people are feeling. A recent study in the *Harvard Business Review* showed that two of the most critical qualities that salespeople must possess are a strong ego and a very high amount of empathy to temper it. The importance of empathy was made clear to me during a conversation with a salesperson who was having difficulty making sales. He had come into my office and asked me, as the sales manager, to cure his nagging problem. I looked for the obvious cause of poor sales: lack of work. To my surprise however, this individual was really working. In fact, he seemed to be doing everything right. He was working hard, he knew his product, and he looked presentable. So what was the problem? I couldn't pin it down. Then I asked him to give me a presentation and do some role playing in front of myself and a few associates. It didn't take more than two sentences out of his mouth before everyone, except him, could see the problem.

At the start of his role playing he had told us that he had come to show us, the customers, how to run our business better. He talked about his expertise, credibility, and how his mission was to show people who were not as well versed as himself the merits of his product. Believe me, it was difficult to listen, but that didn't stop him. He kept right on explaining what a mistake it was not to use his product and to continue using the other inferior brands. Enough was enough; we begged him to stop.

It was apparent that this salesperson's big problem was a complete lack of empathy. He made two critical mistakes. The first is: **Never try to prove how smart you are to other people.** There's an old saying in sales, "People do not care how much you know, until they know how much you care." Granted, sometimes in sales we all feel a need to impress people and convey an image of unwavering confidence and efficiency. That's understandable, but it can't be done at the client's expense. You should never challenge the client's feeling of self-worth and acceptance.

Initially, it would have been better for this salesperson to find some common ground with the person he was selling. This makes the customer more comfortable. It's sort of a "Hey, I'm just like you" approach. "Now, let me share with you what I have to offer." Remember: Nobody likes to be talked down to.

The second mistake unwittingly made by this salesperson was that he put down the competition and implied that the client was dumb for using a competitor's product. Of course, criticism like this puts the client on the defensive, which stymies the making of sales. We all know a salesperson's job is to get an individual to make a change, but to do this effectively you must first show understanding and respect for what the client is currently engaged in.

Case in point: During my career as a recruiter for an insurance and investment company, I would often prospect for potential sales employees. If I met someone sharp, sooner or later I would ask what they were currently doing to earn a living. Of course, all work is noble, but many of these people seemed ill-matched for the careers in which they were engaged. Some had jobs doing hard labor or factory work. I felt they were overqualified for these positions and probably couldn't wait to take a chance on something better. I would say things like, "Boy, I bet you hate that" or "Gee, that's back-breaking work." It seems strange, but instead of agreeing with me these individuals would spend the balance of our conversation defending their present jobs by telling me how much they loved them.

After this, it was next to impossible to get them to seriously consider any change, even though I knew deep down inside they hated what they were doing. It was then, at the advice of others, that I completely changed my tactics. Now whenever a potential recruit told me what he was engaged in, no matter how bad it seemed to me, I automatically commended him for it. I would say things like, "I bet you find that interesting" or "That sounds great, I bet you love it" or "That's fascinating, what do you like best about your job, the money or the challenge?" Suddenly the walls came tumbling down. People started telling me how they really felt about their work, how they were in a dead-end job, how the money was terrible and they wished they could find something else. After they told me the truth, it was easy to present them with a proposal to change their careers. The rule is: **Don't knock the competition! And never criticize anyone's current course of action, unless they criticize it first.**

Focus

The worst fate that can befall a salesperson when giving a presentation is to allow the focus of the presentation to wander. My first big appointment in the advertising business was to call on a large multi-outlet automobile dealer. It was a huge account and I was excited that the president of the company was willing to give me his time. From the beginning things went great and my potential client began telling me all about his family and background, giving me the complete history of how he came to be a success in business. After these preliminaries, he talked about his favorite football team, then he was just about to explain his political philosophy when he looked down at his watch and said, "Well, it's almost 2:00 and I've got to go." He got up, shook my hand, smiled, and left the room. I had been had. I felt used. I had just sat through forty-five minutes of conversation and never gave one word of my presentation. I kind of felt like the body at a funeral: I needed to be there, but wasn't expected to say much! I had made a classic mistake, which I determined to *never* make again. From then on, I would always quickly get to the point during a presentation and stay on it. This may be a little awkward sometimes, but it's absolutely vital if you want to succeed in sales.

Since then I've viewed giving a sales presentation as a bombing mission. I saw my presentation as the payload, and my objective was to deliver this payload to my target at all costs. No mission would be a success unless I hit my target. The more missions flown, the more targets hit, and the more targets hit, the closer I came to winning. Without focus, you'll never achieve your objectives.

Questions

Perhaps the most distinguishing mark of the great salesperson is their masterful use of questions during a presentation. A great presentation is rarely a monologue, rather it's a lively exchange between salesperson and client. Questions act as an indispensable tool to involve the client and expose their needs. In fact, questions are so important, the next chapter is dedicated to looking at their usage more closely.

Humor

Although humor is not a necessity to giving a great presentation, you'll find it to be an indispensable icebreaker. A lot of salespeople employ it while selling. Humor has the wonderful ability to relax a client and put them on your side. It makes people feel good about themselves and about you. However, there are some rules about using humor that you should keep in mind.

Humor Rule #1   If you don't feel comfortable using humor or if you're not naturally humorous, do not attempt to use it. Perhaps nothing is worse than the joke that bombs because of a poor delivery. If you do feel you have this ability, don't force yourself to become a comedian overnight; rather let humor happen naturally and in its own time.

Humor Rule #2   Never tell an off-color joke or a joke that is cruel and at the expense of others. Racial, sexist, and even some political jokes are likewise inappropriate and unprofessional. Always keep it clean and honorable, and if you must make fun of someone, start with yourself. That way you'll never run out of material.

Humor Rule #3   Use moderation. Humor has been described as a tonic, in fact, I've heard of a terminally ill patient who was cured simply by laughing. Apparently, for months this patient surrounded himself with nothing but humorous material, from books to movies, and according to him, this alone effected the cure.

When using humor during a presentation, however, dramatic steps like these must not be taken. In sales, humor works best in moderate doses. Too much and people won't take you seriously. So save your hand buzzers and exploding cigars for the next Shriner's convention.

Finally, humor within limits is a wonderful asset to any presentation, and if you've got it, use it. Like they say, **"Be funny and make money."**

PITFALLS TO AVOID

You've been planning it for weeks. All those months of callbacks have finally paid off and you're giving a sales presentation for a very promising client. You've rehearsed; you're prepared; you've got all the elements of the perfect sales presentation tattooed on your psyche. What could go wrong? Unfortunately, any number of things. This section introduces a few of the major pitfalls to be on the lookout for.

Detailitis or Saturation Bombing

Volunteering too much information is a common amateur's mistake. This is because many rookie salespeople
suffer from "detailitis" and practice overkill. They feel it's
their duty to explain every tiny detail of their product or
service, regardless of whether the client's interested.
They spend their time answering un-asked questions. The
big problem with this approach is that it often obscures
the real benefits of what you are trying to sell. People
who suffer from detailitis usually sell a client in the first
thirty minutes and then unsell them the next thirty minutes by continuing to talk. **Sell what your product does,
more than how it does it.** If you don't, you'll probably lose
the client's focus. Stick to the main theme, and supply
extra detail only when a client asks for it. Above all, once
the client is sold, shut up and close. Remember: Don't
tell them about the delivery, just show them the baby!

When you first start selling you don't know much yet,
so you listen a lot and ask questions. Surprisingly, sales
grow. Then comes the danger zone where you get some
experience and product knowledge. You stop listening
and start telling and sales are harder to make. If you live
through this, you begin to realize you were a lot better off
when you didn't know anything. So now that you're a veteran, you go back to acting like a novice. You shut up, listen,
and ask questions again. And miraculously, sales grow.

Chitchat

The temptation to turn a sales presentation into an
exchange of pleasantries and idle conversation is powerful, because it's more comfortable to avoid issues that
may result in rejection. No presentation stays on track
100 percent of the time, and there will always be situations in which a presentation is derailed or temporarily

loses its way. Being thrown off track by a disruption or untimely question is normal and to be expected. What's not normal, however, is for such things to dominate the conversation and impede the progress of the presentation. Your best defense against a presentation deteriorating into idle chitchat is mainly awareness. When you first notice the presentation veering off course, immediately take action and get it back on track.

Don't be shy about politely turning the focus of the conversation back to your presentation. One successful technique I use is to wait for a lull in the conversation and then politely interrupt by saying, "Well, I promised you I wouldn't take too much of your time, so I better keep my word and get on with it." Such a phrase will enable you to get things back in focus and finish the presentation. When you do return to your presentation after an interruption, don't start exactly where you left off. Instead, *backtrack* and *summarize* the last few points you previously covered. This will restore any atmosphere that was lost and maintain the continuity of your presentation.

Arguments

Another deadly foe to the success of your presentation is the threat of an argument erupting. Making a sale requires your client to make change, and it's important to remember that change sometimes causes friction. Also, people bring all their moods, prejudices, and experiences with them into the presentation, for better or worse. Arguments are so dangerous because they can quickly degenerate into personal attacks. In the event that you must challenge a customer's statement, follow the **Ben Franklin method of debating:**

1. State your case calmly, with FACTS, not emotion.

2. Add a disclaimer saying at the finish "But you know I could be wrong!"

3. Let opponent talk; perhaps they will reverse their stand, acknowledging that your point of view has merit.

Old Ben's strategy for winning arguments is ingenious. It uses reason, diffuses any pride battles, and makes it painless for others to agree with you.

To avoid an argument on smaller issues most skilled salespeople initially follow this tactic: When the possibility of a confrontation does arise, smile sympathetically and try to agree to the combatant's point of view as much as possible. Then gracefully sidestep the issue and go on.

The objective here is always to deflect confrontation and keep going. Only a fool becomes embroiled in a fight. On the other hand, the extraordinary salesperson wins by building a carefully constructed case that thrives on reason, not confrontation. In military terms, this would be described as **a flanking action,** whereby you never confront a strong opposing force head-on, but go around it, outmaneuvering its strength to your eventual advantage.

Distraction

It's difficult enough to keep a presentation focused in a quiet environment, but if you add ringing telephones, screaming children, or walk-in customers, it's next to impossible. So the enlightened salesperson will ensure an environment where a presentation can proceed with as little disruption as possible.

To do this, schedule your appointments during times conducive to a focused presentation. The big winners in sales do what most others are not willing to, which may mean scheduling a 6:30 A.M. appointment to avoid peak business hours. It may also mean scheduling an in-home presentation after the children have been put to bed, so they can't cause their normal havoc. In any event, if you schedule your appointments in less-than-opportune times, you will be at the mercy of interruptions and distractions. What's even worse is the client may begin to view you as an interruption and resent your presence. Strive to ensure an environment that makes it easy to win, by acknowledging the importance of focus.

PRACTICING YOUR PRESENTATION

Everyone wants to be a success and rise to the top, but there is a catch. Everybody may *want* to, but only a few are willing to go the extra mile. **If you want to excel in any field, you've got to do what others are not willing to do, and have faith that this will make you great.** Most people don't realize the price that must be paid to ensure success, and part of that price includes regular practice. As the renowned capitalist Andrew Carnegie once said, "The true road to success in any line is to make yourself master of that line." No matter how great or how weak your presentation is now, it must be improved by constant practice. Remember, repetition is the mother of learning.

The standard method of practicing your presentation is by role playing among your associates. However, if you're alone, don't let that stop you! One of the most effective ways of practicing a presentation is to give one to yourself in front of the mirror. Watching and listening to yourself this way is extremely beneficial and revealing. (Of course, pre-warn family members before you do this, so they don't try and declare you legally incompetent!)

Any good speech writer will tell you that the best speeches are carefully orchestrated and memorized. It's the same with your presentation. In the beginning you should know it word for word and through experience continue to edit and embellish it. Someone once asked me, How do you know when you're ready to give your presentation? The truth is, you're never quite ready, you just have to get into the field and do it, seeing what works and what doesn't. Then and only then will you know for sure whether the quality of your presentation holds up based on the results that it produces. It's kind of like the girl who wanted to learn to swim, so her father bought her a textbook on the subject. It was helpful, but she still had to get in the water.

CONCLUSION

Presentations are a lot like belly buttons, in that no two are alike. Even if it's the notorious prewritten or "canned" presentation, every salesperson will give it differently. There are differences in intonation, timing, emphasis, and many other variables. But the one thing extraordinary salespeople consistently have in common is that they all have the ability to give a great presentation, embodying much of what was covered in this chapter. Of course, no one becomes a great presenter overnight. For that, it takes experience, hard work, and practice.

EXERCISES

A. No matter how experienced you are, humble yourself and give a presentation to at least two respected associates. Have them evaluate your performance.

B. Compose personalized scripts to utilize the entice and withdraw technique.

C. Video your presentation at least once a year. Analyzing this will keep you sharp.

7

QUESTIONS: THE
TOOLS OF THE TRADE

*Judge a person by their questions,
rather than their answers.*
VOLTAIRE

*I keep six honest serving men, they taught me all I
knew: Their names were Where and What and
When and Why and How and Who.*

This is from Kipling who, like most of us in sales, knew
the value of questions. The challenge then becomes to
master the proper application of questioning, which is
truly an art form.

TYPES OF QUESTIONS

It took the helpful advice of many generous associates for
me to figure out how top salespeople were utilizing their
questions. One of the first things I found was that most
questions fall into four specific categories, each with a different motivation. The following section describes the
different types of questions and their usages.

Information Questions

These questions are useful for gathering intelligence about your client. Information such as their background, financial status, and business situation helps reveal your clients' special needs and exposes their hot buttons. It's imperative to use these questions because the answers tell you exactly what to focus your presentation on! Here are some examples of information questions:

Salesperson: Mr. Client, how's your business? [Pause] Where do you see your company in one year?

or   What do you like least about your distribution system?

or   If I were a genie, what would you wish for to help your company?

One helpful point to remember in using information questions is that there are two types — open and closed. The open questions are very general, asking about a mood or an opinion, such as, "How do you feel about business this year?" The closed questions call for more precise answers, such as, "How many service trucks do you have on the road?"

Whenever you detect that a client is superdefensive, it's best to use open questions to get them talking. After confidence is gained you can more easily probe with closed questions to exact the needed specifics.

Rule of Three   A well-known tenet in law enforcement states that when asking information questions, you may have to rephrase and ask the same question three or more times to get the facts. To illustrate this, recall all the times you go shopping for a specific item; when the clerk asks you if you need help, you respond saying "No, I'm just looking." The clerk then asks, "Is there anything special I can show you?" Again, you say no. Then the clerk sees you moving toward an item and says, "Oh, are you interested in that?" You say, "Do you have it in blue?"

The first two responses to the clerk were simply a smoke screen. Only the third question produced true intent. This is a common reaction you'll also experience when interviewing clients. To be great in sales, you have to become a detective and develop a polite but persistent line of questioning. Also remember Sherlock Holmes' philosophy: "Once you've eliminated the impossible, what's left, no matter how improbable, must be the truth."

Confirmation Questions

The motive behind this type of question is to confirm that the client really understands the concepts and benefits of your product or service. It doesn't matter how many times clients shake their head signifying yes, you still must check to make sure they fully comprehend what you are presenting.

This is because, besides not liking your looks or believing what you say, lack of understanding is one of the biggest reasons people don't buy. Confirmation questions act like a monitoring system to avoid this. They should be strategically injected at different points during a presentation to make certain you've not lost or confused the client along the way. They should also be used anytime you detect a telltale blank expression, which adorns every client on occasion. Of course, these questions must be customized to your particular type of product and selling style. Examples of these types of questions are:

Salesperson: Mr. Client, just out of curiosity, why do you think this product works so well?

or   Mrs. Client, what do you see as the main benefit of this product?

or   Very roughly, Mr. Client, how much overall

savings do you think this could mean to
your company in the next fiscal year?

The answers to these confirmation questions will
make it easy to judge whether or not the client understands
what you're presenting. It's always a good idea to ask simple
questions to confirm their understanding; the objective is
not to challenge the client's intelligence, but merely to
verify that they know what you're talking about. Also, if
you ever detect that they don't know the answer or if they
hesitate to respond, quickly supply the answer to save the
client any embarrassment.

By using questions to confirm understanding, you
ensure that when you arrive at the end of your presentation, your client arrives with you.

Affirmation Questions

Affirmation questions are closely related to confirmation
questions, but they serve more as guideposts to allow you
to get instant feedback on how well your ideas are being
accepted. These are short questions that are usually
pinned on the tail end of your thought or statement.
For instance:

Salesperson: As you can see, Ms. Client, this makes our
product superefficient, *wouldn't you agree?*
Client: Yes.
or
Salesperson: Look at this feature. This is great, *isn't it?*
Client: Yes.
or
Salesperson: I really like the way this works, Ms. Client,
don't you?

By tagging on short, affirming questions throughout
your presentation, you'll always know where your client

stands. You'll be able to uncover any objections or uncertainties before they become a problem. Every salesperson should be comfortable in the use of affirmation questions. They should become second nature, *shouldn't they?*

Closing Questions

The last type of question commonly used is the closing question. Of course, the motive for the closing question is quite obvious. Some salespeople believe you use a closing question only once during a presentation — at the very end. Although this is the time for closing questions, the professional salesperson will ask a number of closing questions throughout the presentation, even from the earliest stages. Perhaps these should be called preclosing questions. They don't ask the client to buy the product directly, but merely help build a case that eventually leads the client to make a decision based on the considered path of logic. An example of a preclosing question is:

Salesperson: Mr. Client, you're a businessperson. If you could save a substantial sum off your business expenses, would you do it?

Client: Yes, of course.

or

Salesperson: Mrs. Client, if I could show you a way to increase your market share by ten points, would you consider doing business with our company?

Client: If you could do that, I probably would.

The client may have no idea what the salesperson is about to propose, but if it can be proven that this product or service will cut their expenses, the client has already agreed, in principle, to buy.

So when clients say yes to the main themes in the beginning, it makes it easier for them to say yes and buy the specifics in the end. The great salespeople I know use a number of preclosing questions strategically placed throughout their presentations. This, along with a final closing question, completes the sale. An example of a final closing question is: **Will you be handling the investment with a check or credit card?** This question calls for a decision to take action.

INTERROGATIVE STRATEGIES

When No Means Yes

This strategy is built on the principle that it's important to get people to say yes but it's a lot easier to get them to say no and still win. This is based on the theory that people like saying no a lot more than saying yes. This isn't hard to fathom, because after the words *Daddy* and *Mommy*, the word most of us learn and use as children is *no*. After that comes *yes*, and, much later, after we've been exposed to politicians, we learn the word *maybe*.

I remember one great sales manager who once told me the real secret to success in selling was to go out and get ten people to say no to you everyday. Well, I found it wasn't too hard to get a no response, it was just hard living with it, unless you could get a no to mean yes. Sometimes, just getting a client to agree to listen to you can be a challenge. Allow me to illustrate: You walk into a client's office and he's got a mound of paper in front of him, his arms are folded, and he has a perturbed look on his face. He's in a real "no" kind of mood. In fact, he can't wait to tell you he's not interested. In such a case, why not go with the flow? Instead of asking a question that demands a "yes" answer, try giving him what he wants by letting him say no. Just start out by saying something like this:

Salesperson: Mr. Smith, excuse me for asking you this, but do you like spending a lot of money for overhead expenses?

Client: No, of course not.

Salesperson: That's what I thought, so here are a few ideas that might really help you save on these expenses.

Then immediately begin the body of your presentation. By using this kind of question, you can neutralize the client's main defensive weapon by making their no mean yes. This will allow you to continue your presentation. So it's not bad news to hear no if you've designed your questions in such a way that a "no" answer leads to a "yes" result.

Answer a Question with a Question

Many times a salesperson will be on the receiving end of a question. When this happens, first and foremost find out the exact motive a client may have for asking a question. Why? Witness this case in point: One time during a sale, which I felt certain would close easily, the client asked me if my product came with a particular feature which at the time was extremely popular. I quickly responded, bristling with pride, saying that it certainly did. To my surprise, the client's expression changed and he said, "If it does, then I don't want to buy at all." Caught unawares, it took me fifteen minutes to convince this client that he didn't have to purchase the product with that feature attached. Only then did the deal finally close.

It seems this client had had a bad experience with this accessory, and his contempt for it obliterated from his view the product's main function. After this eye-opening experience, I learned to employ a different strategy whenever a client asked me a question. From then on, I would first discern the exact reason the client was asking me the question before I answered it. Of course, the only way to do this is to answer his question with another question.

For example, after his question I should have asked: "Mr. Client, do you want this particular feature to come with the product?" If he answered no, I would simply comply with his wishes by telling him the product doesn't have to come with this feature, and then continue selling! If he said yes, I'd show him the details of the attached feature, with the confidence of knowing that this is what he wanted.

The fun part of using this approach is that it can be practiced almost anywhere. You can use it at home or at the office. It really doesn't matter; the main thing is to become familiar with answering a question with a question before you commit yourself.

The Controlling Power of Questions

Most successful salespeople have discovered this truth: **Those who ask the questions control the conversation.** For this reason, they try to end every statement with a question. This keeps clients and prospects channeled in the direction you want them to go. A good example of this is found in telephone sales and telephone prospecting. For instance:

Salesperson: Good evening, Mr. Jones. I'm calling for the XYZ Company. *Have you heard of us?*

Client: No.

Salesperson: Well, Mr. Jones, we've been doing business in our community for twenty years. *Are you new to our area?*

Client: No, I've lived here all my life.

Salesperson: That's great, Mr. Jones. Listen, the reason I'm calling is we have a special service, which is free of charge and comes with no obligation. This service will analyze your

current financial needs in the area of insurance and investing. *Is financial planning
important to you and your family, Mr. Jones?*
Client: Yes, it is.
Salesperson: Good, Mr. Jones. Let me suggest a time we
might meet. *Would Thursday or Friday be better?*

In this example, notice that the salesperson always ended
his part of the conversation with a question. This helps
him control the direction of the interview, steering it to a
favorable conclusion. For optimum control in selling,
end your statements with a question and try to increase
your total question count, because those who ask the
questions control the conversation!

A word of caution: The above technique is a must for
telephone sales, but you should limit its use in face-to-
face selling. Here, overuse of controlling questions will
be perceived as too manipulative, resulting in a monologue rather than a healthy dialogue.

Of course, to use this tactic successfully you must be
confident that the answers you receive will help and not
hurt the sales process, which is the focus of the next section.

Never Ask a Question if the Answer Is Unpredictable

Naturally, a question asked of a client during a presentation can bring forth a variety of answers. Some responses
can effect your presentation positively. Others, however,
can have a decidedly negative effect. One of the best ways
to avoid getting a negative response to a question is to
purposely try to control the answer given. A realistic
approach is to try to restrict the overall range of answers
a client could give you. For example, after a presentation
I could ask a client, What do you think? But in this age of
sophistication and skepticism, there's no telling what
kind of response I would get from such an open-ended

question! A better tactic would be for me to ask the client something like: "Mr. Client, what do you like best about what I've just shown you?" This would effectively restrict the range of a client's answer and keep it on a more positive theme to effect a buying decision.

During a presentation, the type of questions you ask definitely can determine whether you'll illicit a negative or positive response. Often in selling, you must be careful to ask questions that limit surprise answers. This must be done subtly and with care, so as not to appear to be leading the client.

The last and perhaps biggest question to ask ourselves is: Are we really using the power of questions to our full advantage? Proper questioning is a special skill that must be acquired to ensure success in all phases of selling.

Proficient salespeople master the art of questioning, which enables them to fully identify and meet the needs of those they wish to sell. **They know that questions are the answers in big-league selling.**

EXERCISES

A. As a group drill, have one person select different categories of questions. Then call upon various members to supply appropriate examples.

B. Strategically place pertinent questions throughout your presentation.

C. Remember: The discovery was not having the right answer at last, but knowing the question that needed to be asked.

8

OBJECTIONS: THE MESSENGERS OF VICTORY

Nothing in life is so exhilarating as to be shot at with no result.
WINSTON CHURCHILL

Have you heard the story about the novice salesperson who ended up breaking all his company's sales records during his first year? Everybody from New York to California was dying to know his secret. So it was no surprise when he was made the focus of attention at the big national sales convention. The president of the company made a flowery speech about the accomplishments of this young superstar and then brought him on stage to receive an award and field questions from the eager and highly sophisticated audience. It wasn't long before the topic turned to handling objections. One inquisitive salesperson from the audience asked the young man what he did when a client objected to the price; another quickly followed with an inquiry of how to respond when a prospective buyer says they want to shop around. And on it went. But, strangely, the young superstar just stood there smiling and nodding. Everybody, including the president, waited anxiously to hear his words of wisdom, because if anybody knew the complicated secrets to overcoming objections, surely this young go-getter did.

Finally, the young man looked at the eager crowd and said confidently, "Handling objections like these, shoot, that's easy. Whenever someone says something like that to me, I just say, 'Ah heck, don't worry about it, just sign here!' Try it . . . it works for me every time!"

You can imagine how foolish the president of the company must have felt. But the irony of this story is that there really are salespeople out there who get away with handling objections that easily. Unfortunately for the rest of us mortals in sales, it may take a little more to overcome the objections we face day to day.

The old pat answer to handling objections has always been that an objection is merely a request for more information. Sure, and I suppose a brain tumor is just a call for aspirin. No, you'll need more than this simplistic approach to successfully defuse the minefield of objections.

EVALUATING OBJECTIONS

The first place to start is, as always, with the positives. Like all aspects of selling, there are definite positives to encountering objections. No doubt the first positive is **where there are no objections, there are no sales.** In other words, an objection is merely a necessary part of the overall sales process.

Psychologists tell us that in a healthy relationship there's two-way communication. It may be pleasant and, at times, even argumentative; but there's always interest present and it's being expressed. The same principle applies for you and a prospective buyer: If you create interest in a client, they will express it either by objection or agreement. But, either way, they are interested.

A crafty old sales manager once asked me this question: **Do you know the only objection that can't be overcome?** Got the answer? The only objection you can't overcome is the objection you never hear.

In sales, the worst possible position to be in is giving a presentation to someone who acts like they have the lead role in the film, *Attack of the Faceless Zombies.* You know the type: no smiles, no expression, no talking, and definitely no sale! It's times like these you'd love to hear a nice, big, ugly objection!

So objections are not all bad, and are actually quite indispensable to the making of sales. The following section outlines three useful steps for confronting and subdividing objections. Most accomplished salespeople, consciously or unconsciously, employ all three!

STEP ONE: *Identification.*

Will the **real objection** please stand up! Perhaps the strangest thing about objections is that the first one voiced is seldom the true reason why prospects won't buy. It seems people don't like to reveal what's really bothering them. I believe that this problem of concealment, and of exposing the real objection, is directly related to the nature of the reasons themselves. Let me explain: First of all, there are basically four reasons why people don't buy:

1. They are financially incapable.
2. They really don't have a need.
3. They don't understand, they misconceive, are fearful, or have drawn false conclusions.
4. They don't like or trust you.

If you examine these reasons closely, it becomes obvious why people are so evasive in voicing their real objections. For instance, take reason #1: Let's face it; most people find it difficult to tell others they may be broke. It's rather humbling. Most people prefer not to say anything that would hurt another's feelings or be confrontational. Of the four reasons, the only one that people find easy to admit is the second one — they simply don't have a need. People also find it difficult to admit they don't understand something, fearing they will appear stupid or incompetent; that explains #3. As for #4, not liking or trusting the person who is selling, well, people are far too polite. Most prefer not to say anything that would hurt another's feelings or be confrontational. The result of all this intrigue is that it makes selling more difficult because it's hard to fight what you can't see. As any good general knows, **the first rule of battle is to know your adversary.**

With these thoughts in mind, let's reveal some methods to expose the true objections.

Method A — Relax, Listen, Summarize, Qualify Whenever an objection is expressed by a client, the first thing to do is relax; the second is to listen. The relaxing part isn't hard to master, but a lot of salespeople seem to have trouble listening. Perhaps this is because listening seems too passive. The classic mistake of the amateur is to begin a full-scale assault against the objection, even before the client has finished voicing it. This type of tactic only alienates clients, making them less receptive. Not letting clients finish their thoughts makes them feel you're not interested in them as much as in fulfilling your own needs.

Therefore remember: **Great listeners outsell great talkers.** So let the clients have a field day expressing their objections. Once they have expressed their initial objection, calmly summarize and repeat the objection back to them in the form of a question with some qualifiers added.

For example, a client named Bill initially objects to the price of a product. After he finishes, you respond by saying something like this:

Salesperson: So, Bill, if I'm hearing you right, you feel
                good about everything else, but you just

want to be sure the value justifies the price
of this service. Is that it?

The main purpose of summarizing and repeating the
objection is to help verify that it's the only obstacle present
in the client's mind. By using such qualifying statements
in your question as "you feel good about everything else,"
you in effect isolate the objection or spur the client to
reveal more. Interestingly, after you repeat the client's
objection in the right way, many times the clients will
open up, letting you know what's really bothering them.
The reason for this is clients now feel quite comfortable
telling you more, because you are relaxed and calmly listened to their feelings first. This process really works in
getting clients to express their true objections, and it's
much easier than slipping them a Mickey of Sodium
Pentothal. Just remember: **Relax, listen, summarize, and
qualify every objection.**

Method B — The Devil's Advocate   Of course, the method
just discussed works great whenever a client presents an
initial objection. But what do you do when a client gives
no reaction at all? In this case, you've got to help the process
along. Here's how: Let's suppose that after the major
concepts of your presentation have been explained, there's
no positive or negative reaction from your prospective
client. This tells you, of course, you're in deep trouble and
also that there's a hidden objection holding your client
back. You now have to find out what it is before you can
dispense with it. At this point you should close down your
presentation and ask the client the following question.

Salesperson: Listen, Bill, I know you personally don't feel
this way, but if you had to play the devil's
advocate for a moment, what do you think
other people might object to most about
what I've just proposed?

The beauty in this question is that when the client relays an objection that they feel others may have, this, of course, reveals what they themselves are uncomfortable with. Once these true objections have been exposed, it now becomes a simple matter of evaluating them and overcoming them.

Method C — The Disappearing Objection Here's a solid line to use when testing the soundness of any objection. After the objection has been stated, simply ask: "What if that wasn't a problem, could we then go ahead?" If the client says yes, you address the objection and negotiate a solution. If the client is hesitant to answer, you now know there is a hidden objection and can use the devil's advocate method to try to bring it to light.

STEP TWO: *Evaluation.*

After an objection has been successfully exposed, it then has to be overcome. Contrary to popular belief, there are some people who simply cannot buy. These people are not merely voicing trivial objections that can be neutralized, but rather are stating legitimate reasons that absolutely prevent them from buying. This is why you must evaluate every objection to determine its validity. If you do find a legitimate sale-stopping situation, it's imperative you change the object of your presentation from making a sale to something else useful, such as getting valuable referrals or creating goodwill that will pave the way for a sale at a later date.

Without question, one of the most senseless wastes of a salesperson's time is trying to sell a client who can't buy. The object is to know when to attack and when to back off. Of course, most of the time you'll be on the attack and it will be a rare event that you retreat. But if a retreat does occur, don't feel defeated. Just remember what one American general said during the Korean War when he was overrun by the Red Army: **"Hell, we're not retreating, we're just advancing in another direction."**

STEP THREE: *Overcoming the objection.*

Once a real objection has been exposed and passes your evaluation, it must be neutralized. The cardinal rule to overcoming objections is to be honest! So if a customer points out a glaring disadvantage and it's true, acknowledge it, then provide advantages that will outweigh any negatives. For example, say a customer boldly objects to your price.

Customer: Your price is too high.
Salesperson: Of course it is! And it drives our competition crazy! (now pause)
Customer: OK, I'll bite, why?
Salesperson: (Now explain your advantages and add value).

You see, by not trying to downplay the obvious, you operate from a position of strenght.

As for methods to negate objections there are as many different strategies as there are cures for the hiccups. The next section examines three of the best. Together these three methods are perhaps the most powerful techniques employed by top salespeople. For an objection-killing technique to work, it must possess at least three qualities: Naturally, it must work; second, it must be easy to master; and third, it must be readily adapted to any line of selling. The three techniques presented in the next section more than meet these qualifications.

OVERCOMING OBJECTIONS

Method One — The Big Picture   Why try to kill an objection when the client can do it for you? That's what often happens when you use this mode of operation. Observe. When a prospect voices an objection, pause, and then ask very calmly, "What does this mean to the overall picture?" Don't say anything more!

When the prospect responds, they'll confirm how serious the objection is or isn't. Plus, if you're lucky, they'll talk long enough to answer the objection and talk themselves right out of it. When this happens, it's beautiful, so it's certainly worth a try. If this procedure doesn't quell the objection, add the next two techniques.

Method Two — Feel, Felt, Found   Three little words: *feel, felt, found.* But, next to "I love you" they may be the most profitable words a person can utter. The feel-felt-found method is a favorite objection killer. Once used, it becomes second nature. Here's how it works: When a client, for example Old Bill again, states an objection, you simply smile reassuringly, nodding your head in sympathetic agreement. Next, repeat the objection back to them, reaffirming and qualifying it. Then, simply say this: "I know how you *feel*, Bill. I *felt* the same way, too, but let me share with you what I *found* out." It's at this point that you share the information to overcome the objection. The real genius of the feel-felt-found method is that it takes away the usual confrontational response clients are so used to getting from overanxious salespeople. Instead, it allows the salesperson to agree with the client and lets them know it's OK to feel that way. By agreeing with the client and empathizing with them, you'll now appear more confident, working from a position of strength.

It was Abraham Lincoln who said, **"If you wish to win a man over to your ideas, first make him your friend."** That's good advice, because overcoming objections is more than just appealing to a client's good sense. It's also showing concern for their feelings. This technique goes a long way in helping accomplish this goal. Perhaps you're saying, "I don't believe it's that simple." Well, I know how you feel. I felt the same way too. But you know what I found out? **The feel-felt-found method works!**

One word of caution about using the feel-felt-found method, or any selling technique for that matter. Strive to never be seen as repetitive or predictable to your clients. To accomplish this, find alternative words and phrases which you can interchange with your regular standbys. For instance, use variations like, "I can relate to that. I think anybody could, but let me share with you this idea" or "I certainly can appreciate your point. I see it clearly, but consider this." To appear natural, get a repertoire of tried-and-true techniques. Then add variation to keep them interesting.

Method Three — The Analogy Everybody loves a good story, especially if it's one they can take part in. That's the beauty behind this next objection destroyer—the analogy. Sometimes the most effective way to help a client see your point of view is to totally remove them from the current situation and place before them a set of hypothetical circumstances in story form. This story would present a problem which the client must negotiate through using common sense and logic. The strategy here is that by arriving at the proper solution to the hypothetical problem, an immediate analogy can be made by the salesperson, which will relate to and negate the objection. This clears the way to close the sale. Of course, as you'll see, the explanation for this is far more complicated than its actual practice.

The first time I became aware of the power of the analogy was when I asked my sales manager why he wanted us to initially say so little to a potential client. He told us, emphatically, that we were to say only enough to secure an appointment. After I voiced my doubts on the soundness of this strategy, he calmly smiled and said, "Barry, I know how you **feel**, I **felt** exactly the same way. But, let me ask you a question. Suppose I asked you to jump out of an airplane, without a parachute, for a million dollars. Would you do it?"

Not hesitating, I said, "No way, no way!"

Still smiling my manager said, "Oh, I forgot to tell you, the plane you'd have jumped from *would never have left the ground!*" So you see, Barry, you jumped to a conclusion—a wrong conclusion—because you didn't have all the facts. It's the same with potential clients. They're also prone to jumping to conclusions without all the facts at their disposal. So unless you can give a full presentation to a client, just get an appointment."

Although I felt a little stupid, I got the point. This sales manager had skillfully overcome my objection by using a powerful and thought-provoking analogy. Perhaps the best thing about using analogies is that they allow your client to become personally involved in the thought process. And through their own experience, they navigate their way to the right answer.

Here's another example: Suppose a client can save money using your product but still resists buying. A seasoned salesperson might use the following analogy to overcome this resistance.

Salesperson: Bill, let me ask you something. If you were walking down the street and you suddenly discovered you had a hole in one of your pockets and your money was spilling out on the sidewalk, would you keep putting money in that same pocket, or move it?

The answer, of course, is obvious. Now a strong comparison can be made between the logic of changing pockets and the equally good sense in changing products. Both will save money. Again, a simple analogy brings to life the salesperson's point of view.

Because this form of objection killing is so much fun, let's look at just one more. Let's suppose your product was a little more expensive but was built to last. Your client objected, however, citing a competitor's product, which was cheaper in price but not known for its longevity of service. How would you overcome this price objection? This analogy should prove helpful:

Salesperson: Bill, suppose you wanted to fly nonstop from New York to Los Angeles and you called two competing airlines. Airline A, noted for dependability, quoted you a fair price for a direct flight. Then you called Airline B, who said if you were willing to fly a certain type of plane, they could save you 30 percent. However, they also said they didn't know if this plane could make it all the way to Los Angeles, but if it did break down, it would be repaired at one of their convenient service centers. Bill, which airline would you choose?

Client: A.

You can now use this analogy to draw a comparison, saying something like this:

Salesperson: Bill, it's the same with our product. We're like Airline A: We have a good price and a great product, which will perform over the long haul, just like your business does.

So whether simple or complex, collect analogies that are appropriate and use them at every opportunity. They're fun to use and, above all, they work.

Of course, the ideal way to kill an objection is to neutralize it, before a prospect can even think of it. This is difficult to do, but there are some talented salespeople who know instinctively what their clients will like and what they may object to. They then gear their presentation to appeal to these needs, even before they are expressed. To help develop this sixth sense, become familiar with the Plaid Personality Profile in Chapter 3. By using this, you can generally size up the type of person you are dealing with, getting a feel for their likes and dislikes.

Another key to personalizing your presentation is to simply ask yourself this question before, during, and after your presentation: **If I were this client, what would I be thinking?** This introspective questioning should help create a more personal presentation, the objective of which is to make each and every client feel comfortable with what you're proposing. This is a skill you should try to develop over time.

A fringe benefit of perfecting the art of objection killing is that it also helps us in our relationships with our children, our neighbors, and even the mechanic down the street. In daily life, there are ample opportunities to practice the techniques discussed in this chapter. No sales skill is more important to master than that of overcoming objections. **It's the ability to win when all else seems lost and the knack of turning possible defeat into victory.**

EXERCISES

A. For a group or individual drill for skill, determine the main objections your product or service is faced with and develop at least two original analogies for each objection.

B. Have group memorize big picture and feel-felt-found techniques.

9

THE CLOSE

You've got to get to the stage in life where going for it is more important than winning or losing.
ARTHUR ASHE

Call it negotiating, call it sealing a deal, or the moment of truth. No topic in selling is discussed more than closing. Some salespeople have compared closing a sale to serving an ace in tennis or sinking a three-pointer in basketball. But no matter how euphoric the thrill of victory, please remember that no one, no matter how good, closes 100 percent of their potential sales! That happens only in books and at sales conventions. Deep down, you know that, but you sometimes wonder when you hear some puffed-up blow-hard tell you how he never misses a sale. Everybody does from time to time; even Mickey Mantle struck out once in a while. With this in mind, let's look at what's involved in closing a sale.

KEY POINTS TO REMEMBER

Never Sell Price Alone

If you want to become a good closer, you've got to sell more than just price. If you don't, you'll succeed only in

147

teaching your client to shop around forever to save a few dollars. Plus, if price is the only weapon in your arsenal, you'll be vulnerable to competitors willing to cut their prices to beat you, even if it means taking a loss. I can think of nothing that stops more closes than the nagging doubt in a client's mind that they might get a cheaper price elsewhere. In the final analysis, your ability to sell regardless of the price is the best measure of your sales proficiency. Poor salespeople rely on cost only to sell and often give away their company's profits. Great salespeople win by selling **quality, function,** and their ability to **service.** They become **value** salespeople and thus become valuable.

Never Overestimate Technique

To ensure we approach closing from the right angle, it's crucial to never overestimate technique and never underestimate the power of the intangibles. What are intangibles? These are things like intensity, sense of urgency, competitive spirit, and plain hard work. Naturally you have to develop skill in closing, but don't lose sight of the fact that success in selling is about 85 percent intangibles and only 15 percent finesse. You definitely need technique, but the trick is to not spend all of your time engaged in its pursuit.

Sadly, some salespeople completely miss this point, believing that the only reason they're not closing enough sales is because they haven't found the perfect system. These salespeople are the type who want to know everything in advance. They want all the right plans for every possible contingency. Unfortunately, this causes them to subconsciously believe that they won't start to sell wholeheartedly until they know it all. Since this is impossible to achieve, they basically end up shooting themselves in the foot. These are the folks who fall prey to every new success system and professional motivator that comes along — anything that promises a quick trip to the top by working the smart way, not the hard way.

I know there are smart systems and salespeople out there; after all, that's what this book is about! But no one is so smart that they can sidestep the reality of the intangibles: hard work, a sense of urgency, intensity, and the competitive spirit. These are far more important factors than having the perfect system and all the magic bullets. The truth is most successful salespeople become great closers because they have an overwhelming sense of urgency to win, which causes them to work harder at making more appointments, which leads to more presentations given, which leads to more opportunities to close. This factor, almost in itself, is what makes them master closers.

If you've ever been fishing for large-mouth bass, you quickly gain the proper perspective on this matter. When a large-mouth bass strikes at a lure, the fisherman will respond with a technique that helps set the hook, securing the fish on the line so that it can be reeled in. It's an exciting moment, but to get to that moment the fisherman may have to cast the bait more than a hundred times, and the ability to persist in this is the real skill. Once this is done, setting the hook comes almost naturally. As President James Garfield once said, **"If the power to do hard work is not a skill, it's the best possible substitute for it."**

In sales we often see people who are way too concerned with setting the hook when they really should be doing a lot more casting. Although technique is a must, don't become so obsessed by it that you lose sight of the big picture. Always remember that **activity in itself produces learning, but learning won't necessarily produce activity.** So don't expect to be perfect, but aim to be productive and aware of the intangibles.

PRECLOSING

The best salespeople start closing from the minute they meet their prospects. This is accomplished by trying to secure an approval on the smaller issues concerning a product, which will then help affect a buying decision later on. Experienced closers will always presuppose that their clients are going to buy, and make positive statements in the sales process to reinforce that belief. These action phrases that imply buying are called **"go" phrases.** For instance, you'll hear them say things like, "Mr. Client, would you prefer this unit in red?" or "Would a five-day delivery date be convenient?"

You'll never hear a great closer use phrases that promote indecision, or **"stop" phrases.** Some examples of these sales killers are things like, "Well, we hope you'll consider our product, if you ever decide to buy" or "Whenever you buy, Ms. Client, I think I can get a five-day delivery date!" Good salespeople eliminate ifs and whens from their vocabulary and presuppose that the client has already bought.

Preclosing and Multistep Selling

The sales process of today rarely involves just one appointment. More commonly, it's a three-step or multistep sales process, which can take days or even months to complete or, as they say, "six months from contract to contract." The following section outlines what generally happens during the most pivotal parts of multistep selling.

STEP ONE

This is the introduction appointment when the client is introduced to you and your product and, as the salesperson, you assess the client's needs. If you're trying to cultivate a new client who is presently a regular customer of a competitor, it may take a number of courtesy calls before you actually get a chance to introduce your product and bid for the client's business. However, once this happens, this becomes the first step.

STEP TWO

In this period a proposal is researched and compiled which will hopefully meet the client's individual requirements.

STEP THREE

This is the presentation of the finished proposal to the client, the acceptance of that proposal, and the closing of the sale.

The big problem with multistep selling is that the sales process has a tendency to drag out a long time. When this happens, the chances of closing the sale are greatly diminished. So to minimize this time lag and speed up the process, you've got to do two things well: get to know your client and secure a conditional commitment.

Know Your Client Whether it's five minutes or six months, when you do get the chance to prepare a proposal, be as thorough as possible in gathering information about the client's specific needs and wants. And remember, what a client actually needs can be totally different from their wants and desires. Here's an example:

A client may need a plain pickup truck for their business. That's logical: but *emotionally*, they may strongly desire a more sporty vehicle. If you propose just a pickup truck based on logic and don't at least try to address the client's wants by offering a more snazzy option, you'll probably lose the sale. It is critical to really get to know the client and cover all the bases. Remember, **research equals rewards** and most of this research can be done by thoroughly questioning and listening to the client. When

you do construct your proposal, make sure it's personalized. This is a must when you're presenting to a group or
corporation. In this situation, have each member's name
embossed on the front of the proposal.

Securing a Conditional Commitment   The second significant step to speeding up the process in multistep selling
is to obtain a conditional commitment. I'm fully convinced that taking this simple step can revolutionize modern selling.

The big secret to the conditional commitment is to
**never offer to do a proposal until the client first promises
to commit.** Again, keeping in character, I learned this the
hard way. It all started after I secured my first appointments in the advertising business. I then gave my presentation with the zeal of a missionary with only six months
to live. Through questioning and listening, I tried to
ascertain the special needs and desires of my clients.

After this step, I gave my clients a basic outline of how
I thought our company could be of service to them.
Encouraged, I found that most clients would then utter
these immortal words: "That sounds great. Why don't you
put together a proposal on paper and get back to me?"
When I heard that, I became excited and immediately
started working on some first-class proposals. The only
problem was, after a couple of months of this kind of selling, I had twenty-six proposals in my hand and no sales.
Alas, like a potato in a high school osmosis experiment,
my consciousness absorbed another timeless truth:
Prospective clients sometimes use proposals as a polite
ploy to get rid of amateur salespeople and, if you don't
watch it, you can get proposal-ed right out of business.

After some guidance, I decided never to do another
proposal until the client first committed to buy, assuming the proposal met their needs. Why waste all that time
and energy on a client who really isn't serious in the
first place?

Naturally, some feel this is just a kneejerk reaction that could end up losing clients, but the truth is you can't lose what you never had, so why not find out early where you stand. Not surprisingly, using this technique the very next month, my proposal count dwindled but, to my delight, my sales soared.

The importance of obtaining a conditional commitment can't be understated, because without it, a proposal is **absolutely meaningless.** Here's an example of how to obtain a solid, conditional commitment:

Client: That sounds good. Why don't you work up a proposal and get back to me later?

Salesperson: I'll be happy to, Mr. Jones, and I'm excited about getting started, but let me ask you something. Mr. Jones, if my proposal demonstrates we can deliver the services we discussed, in the price range I mentioned, is there any reason why we couldn't do business together?

Then wait for an answer. You know the old game . . . the first one who talks, loses.

Client: Well, no.

Salesperson: Good, Mr. Jones, because I know that time is valuable, and I want to dedicate myself and my company's resources to doing the best possible proposal, so it's reassuring to know that you're really serious. Would Tuesday at 1:00 be good, or do you have a better time in mind?

Wait for an answer.

Here's an alternative scenario:

Client: Looks good; work me up a proposal.

Salesperson: I'll get on it right away. And by the way, Mr. Jones, if this proposal proves we can deliver

	what we promised, is there any reason we can't go ahead and do business together?
Client:	No, I don't see why not.
Salesperson:	Great, Mr. Jones. It's good to see you mean business by giving your word on that.
	[Shake hands while saying this to the client]

Of course, if the client does have some objection to the conditional commitment, you can shift gears and try to discover and handle the objection using the techniques discussed in Chapter 8. If the objection can't be overcome, at least you'll save yourself from working on another lost-cause proposal.

Again, the conditional commitment will have to be customized to fit the features and benefits of your product or service. But regardless, it should accomplish the same goal as in the example, which is to get the client to commit to buy if the proposal does what you say it will. So in multistep selling, use the conditional commitment and maximize efficiency.

Keep the Heat On

The next step in the preclose process is to set up a definite appointment to deliver the proposal and close the sale. This is where a lot of salespeople drop the ball. They give a great presentation, get a solid conditional commitment, and then speak the words that ruin all their hard work: "Great, I'll get back to you when I'm finished with your proposal." Such a statement takes away all the sense of urgency for you and the client. It also allows the prospect to totally control when and where the deal will be finally closed; now you've got to call for another appointment after completing the proposal, which just leads to a lot of put-offs and delays. And the more time that goes by from the presentation to the close, the less chance you have of being successful. Be definite after you obtain a conditional commitment and immediately set the time for the follow-up closing appointment. Remember, the sooner the better.

Let the Client Know What to Expect

How many times on the final close have you gone back with a proposal and a contract ready to be signed only to have the client say, "Gee, I didn't think we were going to finalize the deal today. I need more time to think about it." Boy, I hate hearing that. To eliminate this, try to tell your clients in advance exactly what to expect. This can be done after the conditional commitment and appointment for the closing have been secured. You can then continue by telling your client something like this:

Salesperson: Mr. Jones, when I come back on Thursday at 11:00, I'll present you with a finished proposal. It will show you in detail how our product compares and fits into your current situation. I'll then answer all your questions to your satisfaction, and when everything looks good, we'll fill out some paperwork and get the ball rolling. Fair enough?

Wait for an answer. Again, the first one who speaks, loses (or the first one who talks, buys). It doesn't matter; just be quiet!

Client: Yes, that's fine.

Now, you've let the client know that when you come back it's to finalize the deal and not just a courtesy call. Using this strategy, the preclose is complete and you have taken the right steps to minimize any unpleasant surprises during the final close.

Preclose Recap

1. Assess client's needs thoroughly.
2. Obtain a conditional commitment before you do a proposal.
3. Set a definite time to come back with the proposal.
4. Let the client know exactly what to expect when you come back to close the deal.
5. Personalize the proposal and send a thank-you note confirming the appointment.

THE FINAL CLOSE

With the preclose groundwork completed, it's time to close. Like in one-step selling, where everything transpires in just one meeting as in retail sales, in multistep selling the close usually comes after you've received a positive buying signal from the client.

Buying Signals

A buying signal can take many forms. Some of the best known are when a client gets real friendly or leans forward to touch the contract or asks questions like they already own the product. Perhaps they've inquired about a delivery date or requested a certain color. These questions would immediately trigger a closing action. The rule in any selling, especially one-step selling, is always be ready to close, or, to put it another way, *close early and close often.*

In multistep selling, the same basic rules apply. But again, due to the complexity of many services and products today, there is a need to furnish a detailed proposal to the client, which lengthens the sales process. The only real difference between one-step and multistep selling, however, is the time difference. The same closing technique can be appropriate for both forms of selling, which brings us to an essential point about the necessity of a good closing technique. No matter how good your presentation or how wonderful the proposal, even if it shows in black and white that a client would be crazy not to accept your offer, most clients will not jump up and say, "Great, where do I sign?" Remember, people like to procrastinate, and sales don't close themselves; you've got to close them.

Illustrating this, I once managed a salesperson who, by his activity sheet, showed a very high number of presentations given, but at the same time displayed the lowest ratio of sales closed in our department. One day I inquired about this in general conversation, asking him how he closed a sale. He just shrugged his shoulders and with a shy smile said, "Oh, I just kinda' keep talking and talking until the client finally says, 'I'll buy.'" This is a very poor closing technique which I call closing by aggravation. To be sure, the few unfortunate clients that did buy, probably only did so to get our friend to shut up. In contrast, to be consistently successful you must possess a reliable closing technique that delivers a high percentage of closes without depending on blind persistence as its only weapon.

Trial Closes

The trial close is an intricate part of your final closing campaign. In modern selling, as in modern warfare, knowing the true conditions is paramount to success; a good commander never commits his main task force without good reconnaissance. That's where the trial close comes into play. The trial close is like a heat-seeking missile, and by using it, you'll know if your customer is ready to buy.

To set the record straight, the trial close doesn't actually close anything; it just lets you test the waters. The trial close never asks for a binding decision, but merely a point of view or opinion. By not pressing for a decision, you safely keep away from sale-stopping rejection. Here are some examples of trial closes:

Salesperson: Bill, just out of curiosity, what feature package do you think most customers like the best?

or   In your view, Sue, does the enhanced capabilities of this unit make it more attractive than the other one?

Although a seemingly innocuous query, such questions will reveal the buying temperament of your customers. You should be able to see if they're hot or cold, need more selling, or are ready to close.

A good strategy to close is to ask two or three trial-close questions in a row. If the response is positive, briefly summarize using emotion, and then close.

Emotional Summary

After some successful trial closes, it's time to employ a final closing action. Many times to pave the way for this action you'll want to include an emotional summary, which brings to life all the reasons why the customers should buy. The emotional summary doesn't have to be long, but it must evoke the psychological benefits of ownership—like pride, safety, excitement, comfort, or pleasure. An example of an emotional summary goes something like this:

Salesperson: Bill, as you can see, this phone system meets and exceeds all your growth requirements. But what's really thrilling is that this state-of-the-art equipment will play a big part in pro-

pelling your company to the forefront of
your industry. That's exciting!

Naturally the effectiveness of your emotional summary
will be in direct proportion to the number of customer
hot buttons that you can hit.

Closing Techniques

Now that you're ready to close, just what are the best closing techniques? This section begins by looking at what
they're not.

In the first place, the best closing techniques are not
overly complicated. Real genius is best expressed by simplicity. After all, what good is a closing technique that
takes years to master?

Second, they are not too specialized. Techniques that
are flexible can be used for most closing situations. This
need for versatility was made clear to me after I attended
a sales seminar in which the speaker demonstrated fifteen different closing techniques. After the seminar was
over, it was obvious that the only thing he had left us with
was confusion and a mastery of nothing. He had tried to
build the perfect closing defense for every situation, but
as Frederick the Great said, **"In trying to defend everything, he defended nothing."**

Third, a great close must not rely on trickery or
deception. Salespeople who resort to these sorts of gim-
micks are easy to spot; they usually have the highest
amount of complaints and cancellations. Though they
may close the sale, it doesn't stay closed for long, and
they eventually lose their customers forever. A straightforward approach is a must.

With these standards as background, the next section
presents five fantastic closes. These will be more than
enough to meet most if not all of the closing situations

you may encounter. These five closes are proven winners: the assumptive close, the three-choice close, the alternative-choice close, the boomerang close, and the last-stand close.

FIVE FANTASTIC CLOSES

You may be asking, "What about the old Ben Franklin close?" This is the one where you get the client to list all the pluses and minuses of your product or service on one page. Whichever column is greater determines whether the client buys or doesn't buy. Or perhaps you're wondering about the close you're using now, which may be working great. Well, if it ain't broke, don't fix it. This section presents some of the best overall answers, not the only answers.

The Assumptive Close

I presume most of us have heard the news that you have to *assume the sale,* but how many of us have followed this line of thinking through to its natural conclusion? That is, we must also *assume the close.* The beauty of closing by assumption is that it's a method that can be used by itself or in conjunction with other closing techniques. It also provides a smooth transition between the presentation and the close. Unlike some techniques, the assumptive method does not ask for permission to close; it just starts closing. Granted, you have to be bold to use this technique, but the results are well worth it.

To illustrate the assumptive close, let's return to our ongoing multistep sale with Mr. Jones. During the previous meeting we obtained a conditional commitment, set a definite appointment to come back for the final close, and explained what would happen when we did. At this moment we have just refreshed Mr. Jones's memory of what we discussed before and shown him our proposal and given some successful trial closes. Let's pick it up from there. (Note: have pen in hand to use as an unassuming pointer; also keep the contract ready, turned upside down or just under the first pages of your notepad.)

Salesperson:	And as you can see, Mr. Jones, this plan clearly shows how you can meet and exceed all your expectations in cutting costs and improving your company's overall performance by using our service. [Emotional summary] I think you can imagine the relief and comfort you'll feel when you present this good news to your stockholders.
Mr. Jones:	It does look good!
Salesperson:	Great, Mr Jones, I'm glad you like it. Now, what's that shipping address? [Wait for an answer, contract exposed, head down, ready to write.] Good. And what's the company's ID number?

Continue filling out the order form or contract through questioning. I'm sure you've noticed that we didn't ask Mr. Jones if he was ready to buy. Using the assumptive close at an opportune time, we simply waited for a positive response, acknowledged it, and, by asking questions, started to write up the order. It's a compact technique, and powerful in its ability to close sales. All it takes is a little confidence to make it work.

Of course, sometimes a client may not volunteer a positive statement to initiate closing. Here you have two choices: You can ignore this omission and continue to assume the close by asking questions to write up the order; or you may want to ask a general question to illicit a positive response and then proceed with assuming the close. In doing this, it would be wise to remember Chapter 7 on questions and stay away from sale killers.

For example: "Well, Mr. Jones, what do you think?" or the ever popular "How do you like it, Mr. Jones?" These questions leave the door open to a negative response. Instead, point your questions in a more positive direction, for instance: "What do you like best, Mr. Jones? The price or the performance?" Then after a positive response is given, simply assume the close by writing up the order.

When I teach this close to novices, they often say that it seems unfair. They ask why the client shouldn't be made aware of the fact that you're initiating the close of a sale. Never underestimate your client's intelligence! They know full well what you're doing when you start writing up the order. If they're not disagreeing, it's probably because, for a change, you've given them nothing to disagree about. The assumptive close doesn't rely upon trickery or deceit. On the contrary, it is straightforward and relies on boldness and confidence. The assumptive close leads, but never pushes.

We've just demonstrated what happens when everything goes smoothly, but we all know that the only thing smooth in life is a baby's behind, and even that doesn't last long! So what happens to the assumptive close if the client says something negative? Or even worse, what happens if they stop you in the middle of writing up the order? Not to worry, because it's never over until the fat sales manager sings. In fact, it's all part of the plan.

If this should happen, you simply smile (looking a little surprised), shift gears again, and go right into your objection-killing mode by asking questions. First, identify the objection, then quickly evaluate and kill it, using your favorite method from Chapter 8. Once the objection has been dispensed with, you simply continue assuming the close by taking up where you left off, again asking questions to fill out the paperwork.

Don't be alarmed if this process of starting and stopping on the close is repeated more than once. Just stick to identifying and dispelling each new objection, then always return to assuming the close. The end result will be a high percentage of closes made.

The Three-Choice Close

The ease and adaptability of the assumptive close makes it a strong, all-around choice for closing in any situation. But let's add another close to our repertoire, the three-choice close. This one's been around forever and is a solid technique because it understands a fundamental principle of human nature: When faced with two extremes, most people gravitate to the middle. Here's how it works:

Say, for example, you're trying to sell a client a computer system. On the initial appointment, the client has informed you of their exact needs and budget, which is around $30,000. Back at the office you begin the proposal process to fill these requirements. The first plan which you develop, Plan A, will come in at a cost of $28,000 and will meet all the needs the client has related to you. Rather than going back to the final close with just this proposal, however, you will also work up two alternatives. Plan B, for $45,000, is a much better system with more capacity. This plan will also be shown, along with Plan C, which is a super system costing $65,000. This one has all the bells and whistles attached.

During the final close, you will present Plan A in detail, after which you will briefly show the benefits of Plans B and C. When you've finished, use a trial close and, if necessary, add an emotional summary. Then, ask the following question.

Salesperson: Now, which plan do you think, Mr. Client, serves your needs the best?

Wait for an answer! When the client picks a plan, simply agree with their choice and begin filling out the order, again assuming the close. You should begin to notice some surprising things start to happen. One is that a large number of clients will pick Plan B over Plan A; when faced with three choices, many clients will naturally upgrade to the middle choice. Also, you will occasionally have a client surprise you by choosing Plan C! Perhaps this is the best benefit of the three-choice close. It helps avoid underestimating the client's abilities and provides a great way to increase each sale's potential.

The Alternative-Choice Close

Perhaps the most widely used close in sales is the alternative-choice close. The reason this close is so pervasive is because it is simple to learn, adaptable, and it works. With its great track record this close could not be excluded from any complete work on selling. To use this close, prepare the way with some nonthreatening trial closes and an emotional summary. If this goes well, give the customer a choice regarding a feature or service related to the product. The classic example of the alternative-choice close in action is the automobile salesperson who asks the customer, "Do you want this car in red or blue?" When the customer picks, he has bought. Then the salesperson says, "Great, let's fill out the paperwork." The alternative-choice is also a favorite in closing for appointments. For example: "Would Thursday be good to meet or would Friday be more convenient?" The reliability of this technique makes the alternative-choice close the true workhorse of selling.

The Boomerang Close

This is a solid close because it allows you to take any negative thrown at you by a prospective client, turn it into a positive, and send it right back at the client to close the sale. Also known as the concession close, here's how it operates:

Client: You know, we've got children and I just don't like the fact that this car has only two doors.

Salesperson: You'll get no argument here; I've got children and, believe me, I know your problem. Maybe I can help. Let me ask you, if I can get you the same car in a four-door, can we do business today?

or

Client: We love the house, but the flooring really isn't our style. Have you got any other properties in this area?

Salesperson: Sure, but let me ask you, if I could get the owner to agree to replace the flooring, would you be willing to go ahead and submit an offer today?

In effect, the boomerang close works by isolating an objection or need. It then makes the fulfillment of that need or objection a condition that initiates closing. By the way, if a customer objects to price and you offer to make a concession by lowering it, don't do it unless the customer first commits absolutely to buying. If you don't do this, the customer will simply take your offer and then shop around.

An interesting adaptation of the boomerang close is the **buy-today-or-lose scenario.** This is where you make a concession but there's a time limit on its availability. For example, "This price I quoted is guaranteed only today." Of course if you do this, stick by your word or don't do it all. When armed with a closing strategy like this, you can look forward to hearing any negative statement! To be sure, the boomerang close is a favorite for one-step and multistep selling, and it can easily be adapted to almost any product or service. All you have to do is be able to answer an objection or need with a direct closing question.

The Last-Stand Close

No matter how careful your preparation for the final close, you're still going to hear some clients say, "We're not interested" or "I'd like to think it over," which is the polite version of the same statement. Certainly in selling, no two phrases have caused as much grief as these.

Upon hearing these phrases, novice salespeople usually make one of two costly mistakes. They either get frustrated or angry and try to force the close anyway, or they give up without a fight and go home hoping the client may change their mind. Either way the sale is probably hopelessly lost.

In contrast, the veteran salesperson knows it never pays to get angry or show frustration with a client. Rather, you've got to be patient and keep smiling and realize that it's your job to **turn stumbling blocks into stepping stones by never giving up too early.** When a prospect says they're not interested or would like to think it over, the veteran salesperson doesn't believe a word of it. Instead, he or she calmly realizes that the prospect probably has an objection lurking in the background which hasn't yet been exposed, and this is stopping the closing sale.

The last-stand close is appropriate for such a situation. By the way, some old timers call this the doorknob close, because it may be your last chance before you're out the door. Here's how it generally goes:

Client: I'm not interested *or* I'd like to think it over.
Salesperson: I can certainly respect that, because I know
                    that if there were any way for you to go
                    ahead now you would, right?
Client: Yes, of course!

Now execute a false close: put your presentation aside like you're getting ready to go, but instead of leaving, say something like this:

Salesperson: Now that we've got a little time, do you
                    mind if I fill out my final performance

	checklist for my records? It's only a couple of brief questions. [**Use sales call notes**]
Client:	No, I guess not.
Salesperson:	Good. Now be totally honest with me and don't worry about sparing my feelings. I'd rather hear a little criticism if it means we can do a better job for our clients in the future. First, did you feel good about the overall soundness and strength of our company?
Client:	Yes, I did.
Salesperson:	Good. [**Make a note of each response**] Now, how did you feel about the product and its ability to get the job done? Did you feel real good about that?
Client:	Yes, there is no problem there.
Salesperson:	That's good. Well then, how do you feel about the job *I* did? Did you think I represented the product and our company well?
Client:	Oh, you did a great job; no complaints there.
Salesperson:	Now you're sure you're not just being nice?
Client:	No, not at all, you did great.
Salesperson:	Good. Now then, let me ask you this, and please be frank: Did you feel real comfortable with the price? I mean *real* comfortable?
Client:	Well, it is a lot.
Salesperson:	Which means what to our overall picture?
Client:	I can't buy!
Salesperson:	If I hear you right, and I think I do, you feel great about absolutely everything except maybe the money part. Am I right?
Client:	Yes, I guess so . . .
Salesperson:	You know, if I could make it to where you felt as good about the money part as you do about everything else, things would be different, wouldn't they?
Client:	Well, yes.
Salesperson:	Hey, let's talk about that some more.

Confidentially, what price were you hoping for, maybe I have some answers.

Presto! Because of your perseverance, the client just told you, albeit indirectly, that there's a problem with the money. Maybe it's the overall price or perhaps they need special financing; you even might want to just sell more value, outweighing the cost. Whatever it is, you can now investigate the last objection and deal with it. Once this is done, you can go ahead and close the sale for good.

Last-Stand Close Recap

1. Smile; never show signs of disappointment or anger.
2. Agree with the decision of the client. This takes the pressure off. Remember, **flanking action.**
3. Keep the sale alive by keeping the client talking. Ask if you can fill out a final performance checklist to monitor how well you and your company did overall. During this time ask them if they felt good about different aspects of the product and company. Keep volunteering questions until you discover an area of dissatisfaction. This, then, will be the final objection to be overcome.
4. After the objection is killed, simply close again by assuming the close.

With the last-stand close as part of your repertoire, you'll never again dread hearing the words "I'm not interested" or "I want to think it over."

Here's a quick but unorthodox way to still close when a client says they want to "think it over." Be advised: I don't recommend this method for all situations, but sometimes it's a lifesaver and you need to at least be aware of it. Here's what to do!

Client:	I'd like to think it over.
Salesperson:	No problem. In fact, that's a good idea. Would two weeks be long enough?
Client:	Two weeks! That's more than enough time.
Salesperson:	OK, great. Let's fill out the paperwork and place the order. That way if you do buy, we'll save time and avoid delays later. Now, don't worry about doing this, because if during the next two weeks you change your mind, you can easily cancel. Of course, Mr. Client, when you really evaluate the situation I don't think that will happen. But you've still got this option. Now what's your business address?

Strangely enough, some people have a hard time making decisions, even when they feel good about something. I guess they are cautious to a fault. For these folks, a closing strategy like this works well. In fact, after the paperwork has finally been filled out, you'll often see visible relief on the client's face, and they'll never again mention that they want to think it over. Instantly, they have become a satisfied customer who stays sold. Of course, you have to be discriminating when using this close, and you shouldn't try it if you feel the client has serious reservations. Instead, use the last-stand close to handle these. Of course, there are some products and companies unsuitable to employing this technique. Still, it's a good method to know when dealing with clients who are basically sound, but a little indecisive.

Getting the Signature

This can be an awkward time for some aspiring salespeople, and the following pointers should help. First, be bold; you've got to show that you know what you want and fully expect to receive it. In this, the confidence you have will be echoed back by the customer. Second, avoid the word signature. Use all the acceptable alternatives, such as "Let me get your OK," "your approval," "your authorization," and so on. Don't say "OK, Mr. Client, I need you to sign this contract." This can be the death knell to a potential sale, reminding the client of past unpleasantness from their enlistment to that health-club membership they're still paying for.

Instead, simply slide the paperwork over to the client, with a working pen on top, and casually ask for their OK. You can even employ author and entrepreneur W. Clement Stone's old technique of smiling and nodding your head up and down in approval; it still works.

Speaking of old techniques, some crafty salespeople I know recommend that when the customer picks up the pen, you should politely take it out of their hand, checking to make sure it works. Then you hand it back. This supposedly acts as an entice and withdraw, spurring the prospect to sign. I think this complicates the process, but at least you'll know what's going on when someone does it to you. Anyway, after you've given them the paperwork and pen and asked for their approval, don't say another thing until they sign. Then congratulate them and insulate them from "buyer's remorse."

Buyer's Remorse

I'll never forget the time my brother, who was then newly married and living on hope, bought a $1,500 vacuum cleaner. He told me that he and his bride awoke the next morning with a severe sales hangover, wondering how it happened. They quickly remedied the situation by canceling the contract. Needless to say, the greatest deterrent to buyer's remorse is making sure that you sell the client what they truly need. If you can do that, you'll minimize your problem.

Once the sale has been made and you've congratulated the client, you need to spend some time making sure they realize the sound logic of their decision. So rather than running out of their office as though they're going to change their mind, you should relax and let the client know that you admire their purchase. Buyer's remorse can be offset by selling to the need, enhancing the buying experience, and by good after-sale communication, keeping in mind to avoid controversial topics such as politics or religion.

SOME FINAL THOUGHTS ON CLOSING

There's one last area we need to touch on before we finish our discussion of closing. This is attitude. Like everything else in life, your success in closing will be directly affected by the attitude you have toward it. Naturally, you should be positive; this goes without saying. However, there is also a frame of mind that you should develop, which is extremely beneficial to the whole closing process. I call this attitude the nonchalant closer. It was developed in response to the realization that **the hardest sales to close are the ones you need the most.**

The Nonchalant Closer

I don't know why it is, but every time I had a sale that I absolutely had to close, those were the ones I could count on the least. Maybe I came on too strong or seemed overly anxious. At any rate, to prevent this from happening, I started to incorporate this little exercise: Before I would meet with a client I would say to myself, "I don't need to make this sale; I don't need this sale at all. In fact, the only reason I'm going to talk with this client is because

I've got something that can really help them and I'm going to use some of my valuable time to try to do that." Continuing this pep talk, I tell myself, "Gee, I hope they're smart enough to take advantage of this, but if they're not, I can't help that. All I know is that my career is not dependent on one sale. Anyway, I'll try to help this client the best I can, but **I don't need this sale!"**

Sounds crazy talking to yourself like that, doesn't it? It looks crazy, too, especially when you're all alone in your car or sitting by yourself in an empty office. But, as crazy as it seems, cultivating this nonchalant attitude really helps in closing sales. By the time I did come face-to-face with my client, I was much more confident and the whole closing process seemed less pressured and more natural. The final result: more sales closed! The reality is, the attitude you carry into a close is just as important as the closing technique itself. So make sure you're not a bundle of nerves; smile, loosen up, and remember that the nonchalant closer makes more sales!

EXERCISES

A. Memorize the preclose recap.

B. Develop your own trial closes.

C. Drill for skill using all five closing techniques.

10

REFERRALS: THE HAPPY HUNTING GROUND

*Always plan ahead, it wasn't raining
when Noah built the ark.*
RICHARD CUSHING

Back in the 1800s thousands of men and women left the security of their homes and headed for a dream buried in the California hills. Here they were transformed into gold miners. This was not the title they used, however. They called themselves "prospectors." I guess this was because most of their time was spent *searching* for gold rather than actually finding it.

Selling is a lot like that. Most of our time goes to prospecting for sales and only a small percentage is actually engaged in selling. The truth is, in sales our main task isn't selling at all, it's prospecting. Even if we have established territories and clients, we still need to know how to prospect in order to replace the clients we lose and those who go out of business. So maybe we should call ourselves prospectors instead of salespeople! Of course, then we'd have to grow beards and everyone would want to see our mules. No, the title *salesperson* is fine, so long as we know that our real job is prospecting.

173

Remember, the biggest challenge in sales is not how to sell, so much as *who* to sell.

To find people to sell to we must develop a reliable system of prospecting. This system must be able to identify the right market, of which there are basically two: the cold market and the warm market.

Cold-Market Prospecting

A cold market is one in which the prospect is a stranger. Of course, this means you have no frame of reference or influence. All you really have is a name.

There are numerous techniques employed to prospect in cold markets. Some salespeople telemarket using a phone book or specialized directories. Others call on businesses and homes directly, door to door. Still others have found success using direct mail and flyers.

Whichever system is used, the constant aim of the salesperson in this market is to elicit interest and meet people. It goes without saying that it takes a very special person to be successful working strictly in cold markets. You need a strong constitution and a thick skin to endure the high number of rejections you're likely to receive.

If you're good at cold-market prospecting, however, it can be very profitable. Personally, I never really enjoyed working a cold market. For this reason, I quickly learned that the easiest way to minimize this was to get into a warm market and stay there.

Warm-Market Prospecting

Naturally, a warm market is one in which you're familiar with the prospect or you share a common frame of reference that helps the prospect relate to you. This gives you the precious commodity of influence, which is the main advantage of warm-market prospecting. This influence magnifies the impact of your selling efforts, which is why in some lines of selling the newcomer is strongly encouraged to work only their warm market. With this, novice salespeople initially find great success with their immediate families and close friends. But, unfortunately, after a short time they run out of this easy quarry and, accordingly, their sales plummet. Then these overnight selling sensations are forced to work a cold market, which is usually less cooperative and forgiving. If they don't adapt quickly, these salespeople often become discouraged and eventually quit.

If only they had been taught a system of prospecting that allowed them to continuously expand their warm market! **If only they had been taught how to get referrals, which is the key to longevity in sales.**

Without doubt, learning to use referrals is the best prospecting system of all. For one thing, it's quite inexpensive; there's no overhead. Plus it's time-efficient because you prospect while you sell. But perhaps best of all, referral prospecting is continuous, with one referral always leading to another.

I'm sure you'll agree that all salespeople would love to be in the position of working a warm market and regularly having new business referred to them. Well, this is more than just a possibility when you systematically utilize referral prospecting.

TYPES OF REFERRALS

To some, a referral is merely a name. However, a referral is actually much more than this! A referral is the authorization to use the influence attached to that name. There are basically two types of referrals, those that are actively solicited and those that are not.

Unsolicited Referrals

This is when you are voluntarily referred by someone to a prospect or a prospect is referred to you. This referral is most often customer generated. Receiving an unsolicited referral is perhaps the greatest compliment that can be paid to the way you conduct your business, because it's a vote of confidence given only by those who are pleased with your work.

To rely on unsolicited referrals exclusively to provide you with prospects, however, is leaving too much to chance.

Solicited Referrals

This is a referral which you, the salesperson, actively seek to acquire through questioning your clients and prospects. The solicited referral is salesperson generated.

To ensure that you stay in a warm market, you must be able to consistently acquire solicited referrals. Perhaps the best place to start in getting referrals is to realize just how important they are to your business.

Let's face it, in sales when you have no one to sell to you're out of business. So if you're prospecting solely by referrals, you can never afford to run out. You must make yourself accountable and referral conscious: **The act of acquiring referrals must become as important as making the actual sale.**

For this reason, as a sales manager I made it a policy not to accept any sale that did not have a list of at least five referrals attached to it or a signed letter from the client stating why they did not wish to give referrals. This made our department superconscious of referrals and also allowed us to assist those salespeople who needed extra help in securing them. After taking this stand, we saw an amazing growth in our referral count and sales production. You may not wish to inform your sales manager of this idea, but then again, your manager may appreciate the suggestion! It doesn't matter, so long as somehow you make the commitment to get referrals.

When to Get Referrals

Some people like to leave the gathering of referrals until after they've made the sale, getting them on the delivery date or on a future service call. The problem with this strategy is that there's too much room for procrastination and no sense of urgency generated. Such a haphazard way of collecting referrals oftentimes never pans out. That's why the winning salesperson will solicit referrals on the very first interview, or at least at the close of the sale.

The reason for going after referrals on the first sale is to accommodate those prospects who won't be buying from you, so you may not be seeing them again. The key is that although they may not qualify or be keen prospects, they may know someone who does and is. Like the guy who told the salesperson, "I'm not interested in buying a vacuum cleaner, but try the lady next door. I always use hers and it's just terrible!"

First-Appointment Referral Process

Near the end of the first appointment when it has been determined that the prospect will not become a customer, you should thank the prospect for their time and the opportunity to have met them, and then politely ask for referrals. Here's an example:

Salesperson: Mr. Jones, I'm sorry I couldn't be of service to you at this time, but I'm pleased to have had a chance to meet you. It's been a pleasure. Mr. Jones, before I leave, I wonder if you could do me a small favor.

Mr. Jones: Well, that depends.
Salesperson: Mr. Jones, based on the ideas you've seen
                   today, would you be embarrassed to refer
                   me to a few people you know? [Wait for
                   an answer]
Mr. Jones: No.
Salesperson: Great, Mr. Jones!

The key phrase here is *"would you be embarrassed to refer me
to a few people you know?"* Since it's easier to say no than
yes, we made it easy for Mr. Jones to agree to give referrals on the first appointment by letting him answer with a
"no" response.

Closing-Appointment Referral Process

If your first appointment has led to the client requesting
a proposal and it looks like they will become a customer,
you should immediately secure a conditional commitment, schedule another appointment, and explain what
will happen at the close. At this time it's also wise to
secure another commitment for them to give you referrals at the close. The reason for this is, since the first
appointment is leading to a sale and the client is definitely interested, it's probable that this first appointment was
quite lengthy. So because of time restraints and since
we're assured of seeing them again, it's prudent to post-
pone obtaining the referrals until the closing appointment. Here's an example:

Salesperson: Mr. Jones, I'm happy you're interested
                   enough to want me to prepare a proposal.
                   But let me ask you: If my proposal fills the
                   needs that we discussed, for the price we set-
                   tled on, is there any reason we couldn't do
                   business together the next time we meet?
                   [Wait for an answer]

Client:	No, no reason at all.
Salesperson:	Great, Mr. Jones. Oh, and one other thing. After we do business, would you be embarrassed to refer me to a few people you know? [Wait for them to answer no!] Great. We'll talk more about the referrals when I come back. Would Thursday at 10:00 be good or can you think of a better time?

At the closing appointment after the paperwork has been signed, you simply ask the customer again about referrals. You're now in position to start collecting names.

Salesperson:	Mr. Jones, would you be embarrassed to refer me to a few people you know?
Mr. Jones:	No, not at all.
Salesperson:	Great. Who would be first on our list?

IMPORTANT: Once you've said this, immediately put your head down and focus only on your paper with your pen poised. Don't look up at the client or prospect. Just keep looking down in expectation of the names. If there's a long, uncomfortable silence, you may have to help get things started by employing a technique called "priming the pump."

Priming the Pump for Referrals

When asked to give referrals, some people seem to go completely blank. They then proceed to tell you that they don't know anyone who would be interested. You should note, however, that this is seldom true. The fact is, it's not that they don't know anyone, they just can't *think* of anyone. This is where you must prime the referral pump by asking your prospect or client a few specific questions to help them bring to mind some referrals. To assist in this task, many salespeople carry a preprinted **"Who do you know? list"** or what's commonly called a **memory jogger.**

A memory jogger is a one- or two-page list of types of people, places, and even things. By making a reference to one of the listings, the prospect or client can immediately associate the name of a specific individual. This list has questions on it such as: Who is your doctor? Who do you know at church? Who is a longtime associate? Once you have a memory jogger suited to you and your business, it is invaluable in getting referrals flowing.

For instance, if I was working a residential market, I might ask the prospect, referring to my list, "Who lives on the right?" or "Who lives on the left?" "Who would you say is your best friend?" Or, how about this beauty: "Mr. Prospect, if you died tomorrow, who would be your six pall bearers?" As morbid as it sounds, it usually gets a laugh and loosens things up a bit. You'd be surprised at how many men count their mother-in-law as the lead pall bearer.

After you've asked a question and the prospect or client responds with a name, just keep your head lowered and write it down. Don't ask for any qualifying information at this time—just get the name. You should find that once the first couple of referrals are acquired, the rest seem to come much easier. That's why it's called priming the pump —just like an old well, once the water finally starts to flow, it's easy to keep it coming.

If the prospect does get stuck again, you just go back and ask a few more questions from your memory jogger list. You should try to obtain as many referrals as possible, because some will be weeded out when you qualify them.

Qualifying Referrals

Once you're satisfied with the number of referrals you've obtained, you can now start to qualify them. This is done by asking the prospect or client questions that will give you a personal profile of the referral. This information can then be written on three-by-five index cards.

Naturally, you'll get such details as their address and phone number. In addition, you may want to know how old they are, if they're married, and whether they have children. You should also be aware of how well the prospect knows the referral, and any special needs the referral may have, as well as their temperament. Again, you'll want to personalize the qualifying process to yield the information you find most helpful.

Eventually, from your qualifying efforts you will be able to narrow down your referral list to the very hottest buyers with the best potential. You'll contact these first. This is your **A list**; and only after it's been vanquished will you attempt to see the rest. One of the best places to list your referrals is in your computer, using a software package specifically designed for a sales application; such tools are readily available and relatively inexpensive. With qualifying complete, you're ready to take the next step.

CONTACTING REFERRALS

The Telephone Approach

For some salespeople, using referrals is as simple as picking up the telephone and making an appointment. Their telephone technique may go something like this:

Salesperson: Hello, Mr. Smith? Mr. David Smith?

Referral: Yes.

Salesperson: Mr. Smith, my name is _____. I know we've never met, but we have a mutual friend, Mr. Bill Jones, and he suggested I may be of help to you. Now, I really don't know if I can be of assistance, but I would like to discuss a few ideas with you in person. Would Tuesday at 9:00 A.M. or Wednesday at 10:15 be better to get together?

Referral: What is it?

Salesperson: Well, Mr. Smith, I'm kind of like your barber;
                  I can't give you a haircut over the phone,
                  but I can tell you I've got some new ideas on
                  how to cut your business costs and increase
                  your profitability. Fair enough. How about
                  Thursday for fifteen minutes, you say when?

If you're comfortable on the phone, this may be the only approach you'll ever need. If the telephone isn't your strength, however, you may want to beef up your approach with the help of referral letters.

The Referral Letter

Along with getting referrals from your clients and prospects, you'll also want to obtain a referral letter. This is a short personalized note that you can use to help introduce yourself to the referral. Of course, you don't have to obtain a referral letter to utilize referrals, but it's my experience that using a letter doubles your effectiveness. It also gives you more options when you're making contact. Here's an example of a typical letter:

Referral Letter A

I'd like to introduce you to [salesperson's name]. I believe [salesperson's first name only] has some ideas that could be helpful and potentially profitable. Of course, you decide for yourself. At any rate, keep an open mind. It costs nothing to look.

[Signature of client]
P. S.: [handwritten message]

For practical purposes, it's a good idea to have your referral letter preprinted in quantity in black ink because it's an easier color to match with your pen, which the client will use to fill out and sign the letter.

Also, note that the salutation and closing have been purposely left blank so the "Dear Jack" and "Yours truly" parts can be personally handwritten.

Here's an example of a winning referral letter that uses a touch of humor. This letter was constructed when a couple of us got together with the idea of introducing a booklet to educate referrals to our product.

Referral Letter B

> After reading this booklet, we dramatically improved our sex life, lost 10 lbs. each, grew thicker hair, and finally got our kids to behave! It also saved us lots of money.
>
> If you believe this, you'll believe anything. But the last sentence is true. Have fun reading it!
>
> [Signature of client]
> P.S.: [handwritten message]

Again, we purposely left room at the bottom for a hand-written postscript. This is the most critical part of your message, and the P.S. is the big secret to a successful referral letter. After the letter has been signed, urge the client to write a brief personalized message.

Examples of Handwritten Postscripts

> I hope you enjoy talking with [salesperson]; I did.
> or
> Let me know how you're doing and what you think. I loved it!
> or
> I think this is really great!

This personalized touch increases the overall strength of your referral letter, so don't forget the P.S.! This now completes the referral-gathering process. We now have the names, information to profile them, and even a personal letter of introduction.

The next step is to make contact with our expanded warm market using these referrals.

Mailing the Referral Letter

Once your letters are prepared, you can mail them directly to the referrals. The letters will then act as icebreakers, which will help your telephone approach, because when you call you can use the letter as the cornerstone upon which to build your conversation.

Face-to-Face Delivery of the Referral Letter

The final method of contacting referrals is face-to-face. With this approach you skip the phones and the postal service and just get in your car to hand-deliver your referral letters.

Of course, this requires the greatest amount of exertion and planning on your part, but in terms of appointments made, it delivers a high percentage of success. If you have an aversion to the telephone, this may be the technique for you.

Here's how it works: For a business, try to drop by very early in the morning, before things get too busy. Walk in, introduce yourself, and tell the receptionist you only have a minute, but you need to hand-deliver a letter to the referral. If the receptionist asks if you're expected, just whisper politely, "Well, I *should* be!" Remember, make sure you're emphatic about hand-delivering the letter. Once informed, the referral will probably be curious, so when he or she comes out to see you, or you're shown into an office, be ready to say something like this:

Salesperson: Good morning, Mr. Smith. My name is
         _____. I know we've never met, but we
         have a mutual friend, Mr. Bill Jones. I'm
         sorry to drop by like this, but I promised to
         come and see you. Even though I'm really
         rushed for time, I was in the area and at least
         wanted to take a second to meet you and
         deliver this letter from Mr. Jones."

At this time, let the referral read the letter. This, by the way, is where you'll really appreciate the personalized postscript. When they finish reading, be ready to continue by saying this:

Salesperson:	Anyway, Mr. Smith, I don't know if I can be of service to you, and I apologize that I have to be going, but I would like to get together for a short appointment. How about Wednesday at 9:00, or might Thursday be more convenient?
Referral:	Well, let's see. Wednesday might work.
Salesperson:	Great, Mr. Smith, see you then!

You should know that there's a good reason for making your referrals so aware of the fact that you can't stay. First, it puts them at ease. Second, it shows you're busy, and people love to work with those in demand. Also, by being in a hurry, you cut down on those pesky appointment-killing questions like "What's this all about?" and "What are you selling?" So unless there's a really warm response and the client has time, just get an appointment and leave. Like in show business, **always leave them wanting more!**

For residential selling, everything works the same, except you'll probably need to drop by when both the husband and wife are home. In this instance, always try to see both parties and never believe the husband when he says "I make all the decisions." Sure you do . . . Also, it's helpful to leave your car running with the car door open. This will reassure your referrals when they come to the door, that you're busy and don't intend to camp out for two hours, uninvited, in their living room.

No doubt the big advantage of the face-to-face technique is the fact that the referrals get to see that you're a normal person, whereas on the phone they have no idea who they're talking to and this can cause apprehension! It's a fact that it's easier to say yes and harder to say no when you're face-to-face with someone.

Sometimes, the referral will respond so warmly to your presence that you'll have the opportunity to give a full-fledged presentation right then and there. If this happens and the referral can't wait to know more, just look at your watch and say, "Well, I suppose I can spare a few minutes." Then rearrange your schedule and give your full presentation. This is an added bonus of the face-to-face technique, and the better you get at using this referral method, the more this will happen.

OBJECTIONS TO GIVING REFERRALS

No doubt I would be guilty of gross convention talk if I said these methods work perfectly. They don't, but then again, you don't either. I would also be remiss if I gave the impression that when it does work, everything will go according to plan and be orderly. It won't. Sometimes you'll arrive at a successful conclusion and wonder how it happened, considering all the detours and changes you made along the way. However, you still must have a plan to follow and be ready to think on your feet. If you can do this, you should be successful enough to never have to work a cold market again.

Generally speaking, you'll have a much higher success rate collecting referrals from those who do business with you. After all, these people are believers and, therefore, more willing to cooperate. For those who do not do business with you, the referral numbers will be lower. But if you're persistent, you still should be able to garner quite a few.

Of course, occasionally you're going to run into clients and prospects who will bluntly inform that you it's their practice never to give referrals. Don't give up the ship! This is just an objection like any other.

To overcome this common objection, we must first try to understand the motivation one might have for not giving referrals. The consensus I've found on this matter is that the motivation is plain old fear: These clients are afraid they may appear foolish and irritate others by giving out their names to so-called pesky sales-people. Unfortunately, this idea is not based on mere imagination. Many people have been taken advantage of, having their good names used like a battering ram on their friends.

Once you're aware of this fear, you can deal with it. So when a client or prospect says they "never give referrals," you can respond by saying something like this:

Overcoming Objections to Giving Referrals

EXAMPLE ONE

Salesperson: Mr. Jones, I know how you feel. You don't want your friends being bothered or pressured into buying something on the strength of your good name. Why, I'd probably feel the same way. But you know what I found out? I found that people are flattered when a person like yourself thinks them worthy of hearing a good idea. I repeat, a good idea. This is especially true when it's presented in an entertaining and pressure-free way. That's the only way I presented it. So with this guarantee, who do you feel would benefit the most from the ideas we just talked about? [Remember, head down and pen poised]

Another great way to overcome this objection is to use an analogy.

EXAMPLE TWO

Salesperson: Mr. Jones, I know how you feel; I'd feel the same way too, but let me ask you something: If you knew where to buy gasoline for half the price, do you think your closest friends would want to know about it? [Wait for an answer]

Client: Well, yes.

Salesperson: Sure they would. In fact, they'd be upset if you didn't tell them. Well, Mr. Jones, the ideas we just discussed here can be just as valuable. And, Mr. Jones, I promise, these folks will appreciate you taking the time to think about them. So with this reassurance, who do you feel could best take advantage of our ideas?

EXAMPLE THREE

Salesperson: Mr. Jones, I know exactly how you feel. I'd probably feel the same way. But you know, I found the most friendly way to do business is through the use of referrals. That's why I decided a long time ago to only do business this way; and believe me, I'm an expert at making it work to everyone's advantage. So you see, Mr. Jones, if I don't get referrals, basically I'm out of business. So, just this once, could you help me out with a few names? I promise to treat them with the utmost respect.

Client: Well, I may know a few people.

Salesperson: Great, Mr. Jones. Now, who comes to mind first?

With these approaches it may also be helpful to explain to the client exactly how their referrals will be handled. This is because sometimes people have a mental image of you going to the referral and saying something stupid like, "Hello, Ms. Referral. Mr. Jones, your friend, said you should buy this product from me." With this negative image lurking in their minds, it's no wonder they may be less than enthusiastic about giving referrals, so it's helpful to explain your methods.

This became evident to me after talking with a client who stubbornly refused to part with any referrals, even though he himself was a satisfied customer. Finally, I informed him that all I was going to do was mail a letter of introduction to each referral, along with a brochure highlighting our philosophy and services. Naturally, in this case, the referrals could make up their own minds whether to pursue the matter. After this statement, the client became more relaxed, which led him to give me several quality referrals.

It seems this client's initial reservations were based on some negative preconceived ideas on how I might approach the referrals. Once this negative image was dispelled, getting referrals was easy.

CONCLUSION

If you had to pick the biggest weakness in most salespeople's overall strategy, number one would be the inability to prospect by obtaining quality referrals. This stems from a combination of ignorance and apathy, the two great pillars of failure.

Fortunately for us, we now avoid this snare because we have a plan in place to prospect using the referral system. Now we can decide what markets we want to work and how to obtain and use referrals. We also are fully prepared to overcome any objections to getting referrals that we might encounter along the way. Armed with this knowledge and confidence, the extraordinary salesperson can build for him- or herself a giant lead in the quest to win.

EXERCISES

A. Draft an original referral letter.

B. If appropriate to your type of selling, go back to all your established customers and obtain referrals using your new skills.

THE PRINCIPLES
OF CAREER
MANAGEMENT

To handle yourself use your head;
to handle others use your heart.
DONALD LAIRD

In matters of principle, stand like a rock;
in matters of taste, swim with the current.
THOMAS JEFFERSON

11

MONEY: USEFUL SERVANT OR DREADED MASTER

Money is always there but the pockets change.
GERTRUDE STEIN

The great sales managers I've known taught their people not only how to sell, but also the importance of handling money well. They instinctively knew that a financially sound salesperson is a stable salesperson who won't jump ship every time someone waves a little more money their way. These sales managers realize that good financial health produces a happier sales force less prone to bickering and panic as the tides of business ebb and flow. Consider the following questions to test your financial health.

Do you know how wonderful it is to have six months' income put aside for emergencies? Do you know how much easier it is to sell when you're not living from pay-check to paycheck, counting on every sale? Can you imagine what it's like to work because you love it and not because you have to? The wise salesperson knows all these things, or at least has a plan in place to soon realize them.

It's no secret that salespeople are among the highest paid people in business today. That's why they are so envied and sometimes even hated by other, less glamorous departments. The flip side of this ego-boosting statistic, however, is the cruel reality that in spite of their great incomes, most salespeople will end up flat broke. I guess salespeople are like the majority of folks out there — they spend too much, save too little, and run out of time.

Hopefully, in your sales career you'll receive lots of trophies, plaques, and recognition. That's good. But if you're broke after your career has ended, all the awards are simply a bitter irony. I think the real problem lies in the fact that most salespeople view financial success as in the distant future, when in fact you must be financially successful today to ensure your financial success tomorrow.

This point was driven home to me when I went to hear a very successful salesperson who has a net worth of about $30 million. Not bad! Bob lives in Atlanta and he graciously shared his secrets with us. They were as down-to-earth as he was. The main point Bob made was that even when he earned only $20,000 a year, he saved and invested a good portion of his money and always lived well within his means. He also made a statement that impacted my life, and I'm sure that of many others who were there. He said: If you're broke today and are not saving some money, your chances of becoming financially independent are almost nil. That is a sobering thought.

You must be smart with money today to win the financial victory tomorrow. Of course, you may be saying, "But how do I get smart about money? I can't even balance my checkbook, and I thought leveraging was something you did to keep your recliner from popping up."

Becoming smart about money starts with acquiring the right attitude. The extraordinary salesperson will understand that **until you view yourself as a company that you own, you'll never have the focus necessary to become financially successful.**

Starting today, you're the chief executive officer of your company. Your duties will be to keep your company's expenses low, make a profit, maintain a cash reserve, and invest in future growth. Sure, this position may require a little more discipline, but consider this statement: **Strong people desire and obtain freedom. Weak people want to be taken care of and, in the end, become slaves.**

It seems like a lot of salespeople today have been lulled into thinking that big companies exist only to take care of their needs. This type of attitude almost always has a disappointing outcome, because the companies of today and yesterday were formed and exist to pay as much profit as possible to those who own them. Just compare your paycheck with the owners'! When you are working just as hard, it doesn't seem fair, does it? But if you were in their position, you would do the same because if you didn't, you couldn't stay in business.

I'm not saying that all employers consciously plot our financial demise with no regard for our welfare. That's ridiculous. What I am saying is that there are realities in the world, one of which is that although your company may supply you with a boat and paddle, you've got to row it yourself to where you want to go.

Chances are, most salespeople won't suddenly become rich by what they earn at any one company. They can become wealthy, however, by what they do systematically with their regular earnings. Now to me, that's encouraging, especially when you beat yourself up because you're not making as much as your nextdoor neighbor. When this happens, you can find comfort in this unwritten law that you may have forgotten: Most people tell white lies, black lies, and flat-out lies about how much they make.

Wise salespeople take control, but what do you do once you've got control? How do you get smart about money? Let's start with a mini–crash course in finance.

SAVING AND INVESTING

Financially successful salespeople are savers. They squirrel away, no matter how much or how little they make. Saving isn't just something they do, it's a passion, a golden rule that must be upheld. Most of us know instinctively that we should save, but it seems like every time we start, something comes up and we have to dip into our savings account to pay for it. You know — car problems, braces for the kids' teeth, and myriad other annoying yet imperative necessities that make us wonder why we want to be so ambitious. It seems like it's one step forward and one stumble back.

To avoid this, you have to set up an emergency fund by putting aside at least three- to six-months' income for just such emergencies. Once this is done, long-term savings and investing plans can be carried out without interruption.

You might wonder why I make a distinction between savings and investing. There are some important differences! Investing generally involves ownership of such assets as a home, a business, or stocks. There are no guarantees in ownership; however, over the long term, the return on your money can be very good and it provides better tax breaks.

Savings, on the other hand, does not involve ownership of property. Of course, banks are the vehicle of choice used by most savers. Here, depositors essentially lend their money to the bank, which in turn promises to guarantee principal (that's the money you put in) and pay a modest return, called interest, which is the topic of the next section.

Interest

The real power of money is not in what it can buy but in the fact that it can generate more money.

Money has the ability, in its own right, to multiply when attached to the amazing entity called interest. To become financially successful, you must understand how interest works, because if you don't, you'll give the major share of your money's earning power away! Safe to say, many people have lost fortunes over their lifetime because they don't utilize the awesome power of compounding interest. Of course, everybody will tell you that they understand how interest works, but if they did, why are they broke?

To demonstrate how compound interest works, let's take $1,000 and save it for forty years at 8 percent interest. This represents a good past average return on money saved. With nothing added or taken away, that $1,000 would grow to $21,750 over the forty years. Not bad for just being patient.

Now, let's look at that same $1,000, only this time earning a 15 percent return, which is not uncommon for monies invested by businesses. Fifteen percent is 1.8 times more interest earned than at 8 percent, but here is the magic part: Your $1,000 over forty years would now be $378,721. That's sixteen times more money, or a $356,971 difference over 8 percent. Of course, some folks are concerned only with the safest place to put money. Safety is good, but at what price? You may think your money is protected, but it may actually be vulnerable to one of the greatest risks of all—inflation.

Inflation

Inflation is like the rust on your barbecue: One day you're cooking with gas, wheeling that baby all over the backyard, and the next thing you know the wheels come off and you're stuck. It doesn't take a genius to see that the price of everything keeps going up. The real trick, then, is to make sure that your money grows above the inflation rate. Obviously, if you're saving money at 5 percent and the inflation rate is 6 percent, you're going backwards. Unfortunately, that's the story of many salespeople retiring today. The extraordinary salesperson must be keenly aware of the ravages of inflation and seek investments that stay above its impact.

Vehicle of Investment

Of course, with the uncertainties of this world, it's tempting to give in to peace of mind and put all your money in a simple savings account. I'm not suggesting a certain *portion* of your money shouldn't be kept there; it should! What I am saying is that with long-term retirement money, people should look a little harder at all the options now available in the financial service industry. If you don't, your money may not earn enough to counter the ravages of inflation.

One answer to this problem is to do what the big companies do. Invest! When you decide to invest your money rather than just save, the main issue you will be faced with is how to get the highest return investment while exposing yourself to the least risk. The general law of investing is: **The greater the risk, the greater the return,** and the only proven way to reduce risk in investing is to diversify.

Andrew Carnegie, the founder of U.S. Steel, once said, **"the way to become rich is to put all your eggs in one basket and then watch that basket."** In business, this is probably right. But in investing, it's usually a mistake. To ensure overall safety in investments, you've got to spread your dollars around. This poses a big problem for many small investors because they don't have enough eggs, or dollars, to spread around. Fortunately, there are vehicles of investment that address this problem, and many salespeople have found the mutual fund one of the best.

The **mutual fund** is kind of a co-op in which large and small investors pool their dollars. The advantage for small investors is that their money receives as much attention as that of the big players. These monies are taken by a management team of full-time professionals who invest in many different areas of the economy, from airlines to agriculture, high-tech ventures to T-bills. Many funds have a portfolio that invests in fifty or more top companies and various states and governments. Now *that's* diversification.

The logic here is that the economy is never all good or all bad. It's selectively good and bad. While a few companies may perform poorly, others will do quite well. The fund is watched by money professionals, and it's their job to purge the fund of poor performers and keep a high percentage of good performers, which will increase the worth of your investment. Of course, the only guarantee in life is the fact that there are no guarantees. But over the years, the average yield for mutual funds has been quite good. At this time, many growth mutual funds have yielded in excess of 15 percent for the past twenty years. Of course, one year your return could be –10 percent, the next +30 percent, and so on. So it's important to understand that mutual funds are not a means to get rich quick; rather they are a long-term investment with a view toward the big picture. Also, when you are considering mutual funds, be sure to do some in-depth research and get the opinions of various professionals in the field. Take note that no one can predict the future, but in the past, mutual funds have been a solid investment.

Time

Next to a good babysitter and the invention of velcro, time is our most precious commodity. Time is the crucial catalyst that, when coupled with a good rate of return, can turn modest amounts of monies into fortunes. The wise salesperson knows that there are few opportunities to get rich quick and that what's more important is to get rich right. Getting rich right usually entails starting early, being consistent, and not despising small beginnings. So it's vital you start as early as possible. For instance, if you start at age twenty-five and save $1,000 per year at 8 percent, you would have $279,781 dollars upon retirement at age sixty-five. However, if you wait until age forty to get started, your $1,000 saved per year would amount to only $78,954. At a 15 percent return, it becomes even more dramatic: $1,000 per year invested starting at age twenty-five would net you $2,045,953 at age sixty-five. But if you waited and started at age forty, you would have only $244,712. Now that's an unbelievable difference!

It's important to start immediately, even if you can put away only a small amount of money. Do it today and increase the amount as fast as possible.

Remember, you must be consistent. Being consistent in business is what separates the pros from the amateurs. Being consistent in investing is no different. To take advantage of time you can't start and stop like you did when you quit smoking or promised to lose a few pounds. It's unfortunate that wisdom mostly comes with experience, because that means by the time some people figure out the right way to go, there's not enough time left to get there.

The Greatest Concept in Savings

Have you ever noticed that when you're faced with unusually large monthly expenses, you wonder how you're going to make it through? But then almost miraculously you're performance rises to the challenge and by month's end, you've made it without dipping into savings. This is the basis for the greatest concept in savings I've seen: **Performance rises in**

times of challenge. So why not use this to your advantage? For instance, why not start a monthly draft into savings or investments equal to maybe twice or three times your normal savings amount. Doing this raises the stakes, forcing you to increase your performance. Let's face it, human nature gravitates toward comfort, which leads many people to do only enough to get by. To counter this tendency you've got to develop techniques to break this comfort mode. If you have control of how much you make, increasing your draft should help do this. The upside to employing this strategy is that you'll maximize your performance and, in a short period of time, save a great deal of money. Best of all, there is no downside! If you miss your goal, you can cancel the draft that month and readjust it for next month. Again, adjust it with the goal of keeping it above your normal savings agenda. It's uncanny how well this technique works.

This strategy allows you to let time work for you, helping you become financially successful by consistent and aggressive saving.

OTHER FINANCIAL CONCERNS

Taxes

The first of April is called April Fools' Day and brings with it all kinds of humorous pranks. But by the fifteenth of the month, no one's laughing anymore. That's because, as you know, April fifteenth is the deadline to file income tax.

Taxes are one of the most overlooked areas in a salesperson's career, but to disregard the impact of taxes is a hazardous venture. I've seen and heard story after story of salespeople with tremendous incomes who come up short at tax time. It's hard enough to climb the ladder of success, without falling back a few rungs because of tax problems.

So to keep yourself on an even tax keel, bear these thoughts in mind: First, get professional help to handle the filing burden, which is an ever-changing morass of rules and regulations. A good accountant can liberate you from this mess, freeing you up to do what you do best — sell. Professional help can often save you substantial sums in taxes, as well. So let others needlessly overpay on their taxes. Make sure you get qualified help! It's worth the investment.

Another problem some salespeople have is not holding out enough money to cover their tax bill. To avoid this, first determine your tax rate. If your rate is, say, 30 percent, have at least this amount drafted from your bank account on a regular basis. Don't make the mistake of living on false funds that should have been earmarked for taxes. Of course, if your employer holds out monies for tax purposes, the process is even easier. Don't have your company hold out more money than is necessary however.

I know of one individual who boasted that he was getting a $5,000 refund from the government because he purposely had his company hold out too much money from each pay period. Discerning salespeople never do this, because they would be forfeiting the interest on their money to someone else! The other drawback to saving money this way is that it is saved aimlessly and is usually spent quickly. It's far better to invest the extra money systematically each month, where it can grow toward your goal of financial independence, rather than treat it like a windfall at refund time.

Another common tax mistake is not taking advantage of all the vehicles available that substantially reduce your overall tax bill. For instance, individual retirement accounts (IRAs), (in Canada known as RRSPs) can be set up in various investments, including mutual funds. In simple terms, the money put into these vehicles can be subtracted from your income at tax time, so it then becomes exempt from taxation. Of course, things change and these particular investments may not be available tomorrow or may be radically altered, but there will always be some investments having tax advantages. The prudent salesperson is highly tax conscious and will formulate a plan to deal with this ever-present issue.

Insurance

Most people consider the subject of insurance about as interesting as cleaning a brass tuba. But you can't afford to be indifferent when you're buying insurance; there's too much at stake. There are many forms of insurance, and paying for them all will consume a sizable portion of your income. The astute salesperson will make sure to be fully covered, but at an affordable price.

Let's take health insurance first. If your employer pays the premium, the problem of price is solved. But will the coverage do its job, or is it limited? The only way to tell is to check some actual claims made by other employees. If you find that the coverage comes up short, leaving a large balance to be paid by the insured, you may want to consider an inexpensive supplemental plan to fully protect yourself. In addition, you should seriously consider a disability policy to protect your income if you can't work due to an accident or serious illness. These policies can be difficult, but not impossible, to obtain for self-employed salespeople, so don't be discouraged if you have trouble finding an obliging company.

If you're self-employed in sales, the issue becomes not only coverage, but also price. The best way to try to reduce premiums of various types of insurance, like auto, home, and health, is to rethink the role of the deductible (the amount of money you have to pay when you make a claim).

Most people generally believe that the lower the deductible the better the policy. New thinking on low deductibles, however, points out that the consumer sometimes ends up paying two dollars for every one dollar they get back in benefits. So to save money, it makes more sense to purchase a policy with a higher deductible. The premiums for policies with higher deductibles are generally lower, sometimes as much as 40 percent. So if you have a good amount of cash put aside, why not consider taking the higher deductible and invest the premiums you save. Over the long term, it could mean a substantial sum in your hands.

With life insurance, traditionally the most economical move has been to purchase some type of term insurance. Term insurance is simple; it does only one thing: If you die, it pays your family or beneficiary. There's no savings element attached to these policies, but this makes them less expensive. Since these policies are much cheaper, you can afford to purchase enough coverage to protect your family and still have money left over to invest separately at a possibly higher return.

How much insurance is adequate? In case of a death, a life insurance policy should pay enough so that the beneficiary can live on the interest earned by the insurance claim, without having to spend the principal. For instance, if it takes $60,000 per year for your family to live, based on a 10 percent return you'd need $600,000 of insurance on your life. This sum of money, a portion saved and a portion invested, should provide the family with enough yearly income without having to tap the principal. This way you establish long-term financial security for your family at an affordable price today.

Debt

Debt is rarely caused by earning too little. The main cause of this circumstance is just plain spending too much. **One of the worst places you can live is just beyond your means.**

You understand from the previous discussion the awesome power of compounding interest as applied to savings; you must also understand the devastating power of compounding interest as applied to debt. Folks from all walks of life struggle in the uphill battle of paying off a debt at a high interest rate.

Unfortunately, the average salesperson is extremely vulnerable to the wonderful world of borrowing. Salespeople, as stated, are generally the highest paid people in business, and there's a lot of pressure to make sure everyone knows it. High living, leveraging, and "fake it till you make it" are all practices forever in vogue.

Salespeople and companies are also very image conscious. Where a good Ford or Chrysler did just fine a few years ago, you've now got to have a Cadillac. All this image doesn't come cheap. Bigger homes, cars, and offices and more-expensive clothes are all fine, but only if you have the cash to back them up.

You should also know that there are actually a few sales managers out there who encourage their people to be in debt! A top executive with a nationwide brokerage firm confided in me that he liked to see salespeople deeply in debt because it encourages them to work harder and longer. He probably also has a warm place in his heart for child labor and chain gangs.

No doubt, the fear of debt is a powerful motivator, but to encourage this is to betray the first duty of a sales manager, which is to protect his or her people. This practice shows a complete disregard for the salespeople's welfare and unleashes a frantic sales force on the public. This sales force may, in turn, disregard the customer's well-being in order to make desperately needed sales. Fortunately, this attitude is the exception rather than the rule, but you should be aware that this type of unscrupulous thinking does exist.

It's safe to say that anyone or anything that promotes unbridled debt starts from the wrong premise. So to help keep you away from the jaws of debt, here are some sensible guidelines to follow:

RULE ONE: Pay cash for as much as possible.

I don't think there's any better feeling than paying cold, hard cash for what you purchase. Doing this benefits you in a number of ways. First, and most important, it keeps you within your budget, something a credit card can't seem to do. If you must use plastic, I suggest the American Express card, because it requires you to pay off your balance at the end of each month.

The second advantage of cash is that it usually gives you the option to negotiate, or in everyday terms, you get to haggle. You'd be surprised at how easy it is to get an extra 10 percent off when you use cash. In fact, a good friend of mine says whenever he buys something he first asks the seller two questions: *"When does this go on sale?"* and *"Is this your very best price?"* With patience, and cash for boldness, this approach almost always yields a discount. Of course, people who finance their purchases aren't usually in a position to haggle, because they're so worried the credit department might turn them down. The old saying, "Cash talks, everything else walks" is true. Paying with cash might be an old-fashioned concept, but it beats borrowing and all the other financial razzle-dazzle. Plus you'll sleep better at night.

RULE TWO: Learn to live on commission.

Many salespeople today are living on commission, and this in itself takes a special skill. Some catch on quick, but for others this can be a real trial. It goes without saying that some people can't live on commission simply because they can't sell; however, there's another problem for producers on commission and that is the fluctuation of income.

Salespeople working on commission may make just as much or more as their salaried counterparts, but it's rarely paid in equal and timely portions. For this reason, many commission salespeople live a financial "feast or famine" existence. One month they're dining at the finest restaurant in town, the next month they're borrowing money at high interest to buy groceries.

The first step to avoiding this is to secure an operating fund that will bankroll your business. By building a reserve fund of business capital, you give your entire operation stability.

The second step is to set up and follow a strict budget. Following a budget limits your spending, allowing you to save more money in the good times, which will enable you to survive the bad ones. Budgets can work but you may need professional help setting one up. Learning to live on commission is easy, so long as you play defensively and take responsibility to regulate the saving and spending of your money.

RULE THREE: Borrow only for items that appreciate.

If you must borrow, do so only for things that hold their value. The list of items that will do this is extremely limited. Perhaps the saddest story of all is the unfortunates who are still paying notes on items that have already broken down or become useless. Unless it's an antique or rare collector's item, most consumer goods don't hold their value. Why pay even more for them by adding compounding finance charges? If your cash is low, try to buy late-model, preowned consumer goods like furniture, appliances, and cars. There are some wonderful bargains out there, and no one has to know an item's been preowned but you. Why not let someone else pay the high interest and sales commission that's built into an item's original price? Remember: **If you keep doing what everyone else is doing you'll end up broke!**

The one area in which it does make good sense to borrow is in buying a home. If interest rates are reasonable and the market price isn't overinflated, a home is an excellent long-term investment. Based on past record, if you stay in your home long enough, you should make money.

One useful tip is get a fifteen-year mortgage or at least make sure you have the option to accelerate. Accelerating a mortgage is a technique where you pay more money per year than your regular payments specify. The excess monies are applied to the principal and will reduce the overall amount you owe, so all your money doesn't go to just paying interest.

It's remarkable, but a single extra monthly payment per year can cut the time you pay on a thirty-year mortgage by as much as one-third. You'll also build up equity much faster. Please note one last but crucial point: If and when you do purchase a home with borrowed money, do so in moderation. Don't get big too fast. **Ask how much you can afford, not how much you can spend.**

RULE FOUR: Move up slowly, very slowly.

There's always a temptation to spend too much money in order to attract business. I guess in selling we feel that because we have done well in the past, we will naturally do even better in the future. We then rush out and finance an expensive car, a bigger office, a huge computer system, new furniture, and, of course, a giant luxury home to entertain in, all on the blind hope that this will somehow generate more income. But ever heard of a downturn? What about business cycles? Just ask the oil folks in Texas if a good thing lasts forever. You'll be a lot safer and happier if you first build your business on a sound basis before adding all the unnecessary so-called necessities. Confucius said, "When prosperity comes, do not use all of it." Believe me, there's wisdom in this philosophy.

An owner of a large mortgage company told me that most bankruptcies in recent years have come from self-employed owners and salespeople. These people made substantial amounts of cash for a couple of years and financed everything in sight, all with the belief that they would make even more. Things looked good for a while, but like it always does, a downturn came and their lives fell apart like a house of cards.

Any bozo can drive an expensive car, wear the best clothes, and be the newcomer to the oldest country club in town. That's not much of a trick; all it takes is 10 percent down, and you have the right to struggle with high payments for the rest of your life. On the other hand, it takes a cleverness and a little discipline to protect yourself from the boom-and-bust cycle of doing business. Winning salespeople understand that **real business success is not measured by what you owe, but only by what you own.** So before you add anything or make an expansion, delay your move as long as possible and consider things carefully. Make sure that what you're doing isn't just keeping up with the keeper-uppers. Remember, the quickly acquired facade of success isn't nearly as satisfying or steadfast as the rock-solid real thing. So the next time your nemesis drives up in his or her luxury car and you know they can't afford it, don't get rattled; you're on the right track. Remember, move up slowly.

The bottom line is that in order to be truly successful in sales, you've also got to be a winner in handling your money. Remember: **Smart salespeople don't end up broke.**

EXERCISE

Make as much effort to appear broke as you have to appear wealthy.

12

SERVICE: YOUR PROMISE IN ACTION

When you cease to make a
contribution you begin to die!
ELEANOR ROOSEVELT

Everything you do in your sales career will come back either to bless you or to haunt you. Putting things into this perspective helps you realize that there are no idle actions. This is particularly true when you examine the consequences of service in selling. I believe it's safe to say that the sales world has spent a disproportionate amount of time teaching its young how to get new clients; however, very little is ever said about how to keep them. I guess, like in any relationship, the sexy part is the hunt and capture. Bear in mind that it takes five to ten times more effort to generate new clients than to keep and satisfy a current client base. So the biggest rewards by far will go to those who not only start a relationship, but sustain it over the long haul. If salespeople can do this, they will see their client base and income consistently grow. They will also compound the fruits of their efforts and enjoy the privilege of repeat sales. All this adds stability to their careers. So let's talk service.

PRIORITY ONE: COMMUNICATION

American Express, the financial giant, has often been cited as a leader when it comes to service excellence. In studying what American Express does to earn such acclaim, it becomes clear that they put a high premium on constant communication with their customers. In the words of an American Express vice president, "We try to bury our customers with mail." This emphasis on communication is often seen in their phone rooms, where it's a policy to never let a phone ring more than three times before it's answered. They follow the axiom that **a customer must never be treated like they're an interruption.** In addition, every customer receives a personal telephone call on a regular basis just to check their level of satisfaction. Needless to say, American Express has built a great customer support system. Whether or not your company has a support system of equal quality, there's nothing stopping you from striving to provide excellent service to your clients. Regular communication is the place to start.

One area where salespeople often miss the corporate yacht is in returning messages. Experienced salespeople realize that the way they return messages can either solidify their business or weaken it. That's why they try to return messages as quickly as possible, which means 80 percent of all messages within one hour and the rest no later than two hours. And under no circumstances should voice mail systems be allowed to fill up. Also, when they make contact they display the right demeanor by showing real enthusiasm for an opportunity to help their clients. To further enhance communication, it's a good idea to give your clients an occasional courtesy call just to discuss how they are doing. This practice can defuse minor problems before they grow into explosive situations. Regular communication is a great opportunity to build goodwill with clients.

While I was writing this my young daughter was having a birthday. Of course, she was excited about receiving gifts and cards from friends and family. What surprised me was how proud she felt after receiving one particular birthday greeting. With some dramatic flair, she read the card at the dinner table. It said, in typical, hokey Hallmarkian fashion, "Tosha, the word is out. The news is something to roar about. It makes everybody want to stand and shout, 'Happy 11th Birthday,' your friend, the Delta Air lion." Upon hearing this I rolled my eyes, but I saw how important my daughter felt and this made me feel good. That day Delta Air Lines probably made themselves a new customer, my daughter, plus helped keep an old customer, me. Needless to say, in a salesperson/client relationship, every point of contact represents an opportunity for present and future growth.

Say Yes

The great companies and their salespeople have the talents to meet new and foreign challenges at lightning speed. In order to do this, they sometimes must sacrifice their known structures and traditions. They have found that in order to react quickly and meet the ever-changing needs of clients, they must develop a **yes and a can-do attitude.** Then they say what they'll do and do what they say! On the other hand, some companies and salespeople become so enslaved to self-imposed rules that they spend most of their time concentrating on what they *can't* do. Consequently, they are less than obliging when their client asks for something even marginally out of the ordinary. This attitude will eventually annoy the client to the point that they'll have no second thoughts about changing to a more cooperative competitor. So the idea is to always remain pliable and willing to adapt to meet all your clients' needs. They are the purpose of your work, not an interruption of it. Make up your mind early that you are going to say yes to your clients as much as possible and be prepared to do the impossible. Nothing makes clients feel more special than knowing that you broke with convention and moved heaven and earth to accommodate them. This will endear you to your clients and virtually close the door on your competition. When it comes to service, this is the time you want to be known as a yes-man and a yes-woman!

By the same token, when you are accommodating a customer on a difficult request, it doesn't hurt to let them know that it cost you to help them. This must be done subtly, however, without showing any regret. For example, "Bill, you're gonna love this. I was able to move that delivery date way up, like you asked. I stayed late and talked to Joe Green in delivery, cashing in a few favors. The result is, he's gonna do it."

Showing the effort you made this way builds gratitude and positive indebtedness in your customers. To quote department-store founder Marshall Field, **"Goodwill is the one and only asset the competition cannot undersell or destroy."**

Paperwork

Like it or not, you can't take care of your clients properly if you don't keep good records. I've known a lot of salespeople over the years and, from close observation, paperwork is not usually their strong point. In fact, most salespeople have record-keeping skills on a level somewhere between limestone and a baboon. (Sorry, but it's the truth.) So what do we do about it? Well, like they say, "The main thing is always keep the main thing the main thing." As a salesperson you have a remarkable gift, the gift of persuasion. For many, this gift is worth hundreds of dollars per hour. So it makes absolutely no sense to become involved in filing, bookkeeping, and staring at computer screens. These activities sap your strength and keep you from doing what you do best — selling. So the fact that you're not great at paperwork is nothing to be ashamed of. But never allow this weakness to be seen by others. Instead, contract the work out to professionals. This will free up your time to engage exclusively in selling, while still producing first-class paperwork and record keeping. Doing this will also baffle most of your associates and definitely put you a cut above the average salesperson. Of course, many companies employ a good support system to cope with paperwork; if that's your situation, utilize this help to the fullest. However, if you are self-employed or your company does not have sales support, you'll find plenty of part-time professionals out there who can be employed to fit your schedule and budget. Always keep in mind that the money spent in this area is an investment which will increase your selling and service time to your customers.

HANDLING COMPLAINTS

When I first started in advertising, I handled the newspaper ads for a big furniture chain. One of the owners, who I will call Joey David, was the type who loved to have his name and picture appear in his promotions. This guy was a real piece of work. Joey was a classic participator type and was one of the funniest and most original characters I've ever met. At the time, one of his biggest stores was experiencing a terrible slump. This was because the main thoroughfare they were located on was under construction. Joey had the great idea of running a series of full-page ads in the metro market, making light of this dilemma. His idea was to have his picture, Joey David, on the right-hand corner of the page and on the left a scene depicting men and machines constructing a new road. Under these large pictures would go bold type that read: "Joey David, hard to get to, but easy to deal with." Well, when the ad hit the streets in the big Sunday edition, it read instead, "Joey David, easy to get to, but hard to deal with." Needless to say my phone rang bright and early Sunday with a call from Mr. David.

Fortunately, he saw the humor in this blunder, especially after we apologized and credited his account. The reason I share this humorous story with you is because it points to the necessity for salespeople to be able to resolve customer complaints. In any relationship, there are bound to be times of conflict and disagreement which must be resolved. This is vital because the alternative is so nasty, with every unsatisfied customer influencing others. Remember, it's a small world, especially in industries where everyone knows everyone. Which brings us to the process of resolving complaints.

React Quickly

The biggest key to handling complaints is to react quickly. What seems to get salespeople in trouble the most is not the complaint, but rather a slow response time. Understandably, none of us likes criticism or conflict, and that may be the reason why some are so reluctant to face complaints expediently. But the best course of action to solving any problem is usually facing it head-on. Believe it or not, most customers don't expect perfection from you or your product. What they do expect from you is as much enthusiasm after the sale as you had before. I suppose the problem arises because, unlike the initial sale where there is an immediate benefit, when handling complaints the rewards mostly come later. Consequently, the connection is sometimes not made between good service and future business generated. Outwardly, handling a complaint can seem like a low priority, especially when compared to the financial rewards of closing a new sale. This is extremly short-term thinking, however. The truth is, handling a complaint is a golden opportunity to show your customers how much you care, how efficient you are, and that you can be trusted with handling new business this year and next.

Resolving complaints promptly will build a good reputation in business and spawn numerous referrals. This is especially true whenever a client cancels their business with you. Often an immediate call from you or your manager can turn the situation around. So whenever a complaint surfaces, contact your customers immediately. Remember: The longer you wait, the more trouble you'll cause them and you. With a slow response, even once the problem is fixed, you'll get no credit for it, just bad feelings. So always react quickly!

Admit Your Mistakes

If you make a mistake and your client complains about it, don't try to gloss over your error or pass the buck. People despise cover-ups. They also have little tolerance for those who aren't big enough to admit they have screwed up. Safe to say you'll do a lot better if you accept responsibility and apologize for your mistake right up front. This will probably stun most customers and diffuse any condemnation. This is because most clients are more used to salespeople becoming superdefensive whenever a complaint is voiced against them. Naturally, with this reaction the clients feel they have to act superoffensive to get any action. Remember, reasonable people can handle your imperfections, especially if they know you're aware of them. It's hypocrisy and pride that clients most disdain. So show your humanity, admit your mistake, apologize, and fix the problem quickly.

Handling Abuse

When responding to a complaint, there's always the chance you will have to endure some abuse. This happens, even if you have taken all the right steps to handle the complaint. People differ in the way they handle pressure and frustration. Some people, no matter what the circumstances, are always diplomatic, easygoing, and under control. Others have hair-trigger temperaments that set off displays of anger, rage, and downright nastiness.

If you have a client who responds this way, first, don't resist, and try not to judge your client on one emotional outburst. You don't know the situation; it could be devastating and they're just letting off a little steam in your direction. I've had a few customers lose their composure this way and, at the time, their response seemed totally out of proportion to the severity of the problem. The good news was, because I didn't react in kind, they usually came back and apologized for their conduct. As the saying goes, "Everybody's a jerk for two minutes a day, the trick is not to exceed the limit." After such an episode, I always found these clients to be extremely reasonable.

Of course, there is another type of client. The habitual abuser. This type is rare and very unpleasant, unless dealt with properly. Habitual abusers are easy to spot, for they become angry on a regular basis. With this anger comes a rash of cursing, derogatory slurs, and insults. With habitual abusers, this becomes a regular event and, instead of feeling badly about such a display, they will continue to behave this way at every opportunity, making you their personal punching bag. If you allow this to recur, the habitual abuser will see your lack of resistance as weakness and will start punching you at every opportunity, complaint or no complaint. For these types, the best course of action is a strong show of strength. Once you have identified a habitual abuser, you should, at the earliest opportunity, politely but firmly let this client know you are not required to put up with this behavior, and if it doesn't cease immediately, you will terminate your dealings with them that day.

This may seem harsh and risky, but usually an abusive personality will only prey on the weak and will back down from a controlled show of strength. After all, with such a personality, a habitual abuser is likely to have few friends or colleagues who will deal with them regularly. Once they have been challenged, they will usually see reason and check their behavior. In serving our clients, we want to go the extra mile, but not at the expense of our dignity. As Eleanor Roosevelt said, **"No one can make you feel inferior without your consent."** Oblige your clients but never forfeit your honor.

Satisfy the Client

After all's been said and done, the client must feel satisfied that their complaint has been settled fairly. To accomplish this, you must view the situation from the client's perspective. To make any sales business run effectively, what you are selling must be good for the client, the company, and the salesperson. However, the most important part of this triad is always the client. If they have a complaint about you, your company, or your product's performance, above all, ask the client first for specifics on how you can rectify the problem. Many times you will find that by going to the client first and asking what it would take to satisfy them, you will save time and money, because often the client's requests will be quite easy to fulfill. In fact, it may be a lot less costly than what you were willing to first offer. All they may want is a replacement part or perhaps a small credit. Knowing this up front, you can fulfill the client's request plus, without worry, give them even more to help solidify your relationship, long term.

If the client requests compensation that is unreasonable, however, you can then negotiate, acting as a mediator between the client and your company or manufacturer. With this approach, alternatives can then be presented that will hopefully satisfy the client. On this point, it is critical not to be narrow-minded and chase pennies while throwing away future dollars. Of course, sometimes, when you are facing a large credit for a customer, it's better to spread it out over time, giving discounts on future business until the credit is worked off. That way you satisfy the client, secure future business, and minimize the effect of the credit on your company's cash flow.

In handling complaints, it's important not just to do the right thing, but also that the *client perceive* you have done the right thing. So make sure that client complaints have been thoroughly resolved to the client's satisfaction. That way you won't have to deal with bigger problems down the road. What salespeople have to understand is that being a good closer does not necessarily make you a great salesperson; gone are the days of "wham-bam-thank-you" selling. What makes the professional and top-notch salespeople of today is not just their ability to get a client, but their determination to keep a client through constant, courteous, old-fashioned service.

EXERCISE

Expand your current customer file to include more biographical information, such as birthdays, family member names, and personal needs and interests.

13

THE QUEST FOR MANAGEMENT

Leadership is the art of getting someone else to do something you want done because they want to do it.
DWIGHT EISENHOWER

I once heard a preacher say "you should work like everything depends on you, pray like everything depends on the Almighty, and make sure to watch out for the trucks." It's easy to see the good sense in the first part of the statement, but that last part is a little bit vague. What exactly did he mean "watch out for the trucks"? After personally seeing a few hit-and-run accidents in business, I believe that the trucks are the problems, or challenges if you prefer, that can come from nowhere and sideline a salesperson's career.

Of course, the amazing thing about these problems is they're a lot like weeds. We never have to cultivate them, they just come up on their own. As a youth I fondly recall my father putting this issue in perspective while driving me home from school. I was engaged in some nonstop complaining about some earth-shattering situation I was facing; I don't recall exactly what it was, but it could have been the high cost of tennis strings or maybe it was something to do with an English assignment. Anyway, at a carefully chosen moment he stopped the car and said, "Son, how would you like to never have another problem in this world?"

I said, "Boy, that would be great!"

He then smiled and said, "Okay, then, just go and join all your friends resting over there. They don't have a problem in this world." Of course, he had stopped next to a graveyard. Needless to say, he made his point. So to me, the trucks are the challenges we all face, and in this life, they're unavoidable. The important thing is how we deal with these situations, so we don't get run over.

CHASING THE MANAGEMENT CARROT

In the sales business there's one challenge that's rarely discussed but which has been responsible for more than its share of hurt, bitterness, and bad decision making: the quest for management. In North America, and Europe to a lesser extent, there is a great distinction made between management and nonmanagement. This has fostered the perception that you're really not a success until you've been promoted past labor. Interestingly, the Japanese, although hardly perfect in their system, seem to have a more healthy outlook on employees and management, giving almost equal importance to both groups.

Not surprisingly, companies that are recruiting sales-people for their European and North American markets are keenly aware of how important this opportunity for management is to their prospective sales employees. With this thought in mind, they usually vigorously promote the possibility of upward mobility into management as a future reward. This conditional offer is a powerful incentive that induces many novice and veteran salespeople to become employees. This is what I call **chasing the man-**

agement carrot. Of course, in itself there's nothing wrong with pursuing management. The problem arises when you realize that there are an abundance of chasers and a limited amount of carrots. Naturally, there are many wonderful success stories; combined with these, however, are far too many tales of top salespeople almost ruining their careers by not handling the pursuit of management properly. Statistics have shown that, on average, only about 12 percent of salespeople have the ability to become great managers. The relevance of this number is in finding out where you stand and where you will be most happy. Truly, there are few situations in life more lamentable than expecting yourself (or someone else) to perform a task you're really not suited for. The truth is, if you're good at something, you'll enjoy it. And enjoying what you do is critical to your overall happiness.

The Big Mistake

The big mistake some salespeople make is thinking that excellent personal sales production automatically qualifies them for a management position. But if personal performance were the only key to management, every great athlete would also become a great coach. Obviously, that's just not true. Babe Ruth, for instance, was the undisputed king of baseball for a decade, and near the end of his playing days he was obsessed with becoming a big-league coach and manager. When given the chance, however, he gave a very lackluster performance in this second career. The problem lay in the fact that the skills it takes to become a great coach are far different than those required to be a great player. This truth also applies to selling.

In selling, it's important what you do; in sales management, however, it's not so much what you do as what you inspire others to do! In fact, some say the most dangerous day in a company's life is when they promote their top sales producer to management, because on that day the company risks losing two good people, the top sales producer and the manager who left. So if you're going to pursue management as a goal, it's critical that you have confidence that you'll be able to perform the task well. Such confidence comes from knowledge about what you're getting into. With this in mind, the following section outlines some of the qualities great managers possess. This may be a helpful guide for anyone exploring their management potential.

QUALITIES OF GREAT MANAGERS

A Servant's Heart

The real paradox of leadership is the higher your position, the more service-oriented you must become. One of the best leaders I've ever known leads a multimillion-dollar sales and marketing force from Baton Rouge, Louisiana. He once told me, *"If you ever get too big to get down, you better get out."*

"Getting down" is a fundamental aspect of great management. A real leader must sacrifice his or her time and energy to helping others become successful, and that's not a nine-to-five job. Doctor D. L. Moody, the great preacher and educator, said, **"The measure of a person is not the number of his servants, but in the number of people whom he serves."**

Without question there are many brilliant salespeople quite capable of seeing to their own success, but in the role of manager, they become totally frustrated trying to help others become successful. These free spirits don't get any joy coaching on the sideline. These are players — and there's nothing wrong with that — so long as they play and are not forced or enticed to coach. Being a manager is a vocation in which you can be called upon at any time of the day or night. Like any good coach, good managers win only if the team wins; they then give the glory to the players. Likewise, if the team loses, they personally take the blame. Management is leadership and it requires a deemphasis of the self; it requires a "we" and not an "I" orientation. Before making such a commitment, you must be sure you want the responsibility and that you'll be happy with it.

Tolerance

Tolerance is that special quality we expect everyone else to have when dealing with us, and tolerance is a key quality in good management. Consider what the outcome of World War II might have been if Allied Commander Dwight Eisenhower hadn't put up with the colorful yet highly controversial General Patton, or the brilliant but headstrong British General Montgomery? And what if Abraham Lincoln had expected perfection from his novice, Gen. Ulysses S. Grant, who apparently had a drinking problem? History is full of great examples of tolerance. But better still, think of your own history. Think of the mess you'd be in if your manager hadn't gone to bat for you after that big screwup you made. (By the way, if you're so new to sales that you haven't made a major mistake, don't feel left out; your time will come.)

Many people have the misconception that the main job of a manager is to tell other people what their problems are whenever they see them, taking to heart Mark Twain's statement that "Nothing so needs reforming as other people's habits." But actually, in dealing with people a real leader must many times overlook the weaknesses and idiosyncracies of others in order to focus on their strengths! All with the goal of helping the team win.

The manager's tools of the trade are his or her sales team, and there aren't any perfect people in the world. I like Kipling's outlook on people. He said, "I always prefer to believe the best of everybody; it saves a lot of trouble." This outlook doesn't mean you become a pushover in management and turn a blind eye to bad behavior or poor performance; but merely try to accept people for what they are. It doesn't mean that you must always agree with people; certainly there are times when you strongly disagree. The art, as they say, is to disagree without becoming disagreeable.

In dealing with people, always motivate others to greatness, but never be shocked at the frailty of the human being.

Tolerance is not an attribute of the thin-skinned or the self-righteous. It is, however, the mark of a great manager.

Courage

It is doubtful you'll ever be asked to charge a machine-gun nest single-handedly, although I must admit I've felt exactly that way on some sales calls. It's also doubtful you'll ever be asked to save someone from a burning skyscraper; however, I will guarantee that in management you'll sometimes feel like you're part of the Flying Walenda's high-wire act. Management is definitely not for the faint-hearted. The decisions are usually bigger, affecting more people, and the wrong decision can affect your whole career. It takes courage to be a good manager, the courage to take the blame for others' performances when things aren't going well. It takes courage to call a shot and stand by it in the face of criticism. It takes courage to wear a smile when the going gets tough. *Webster's New Collegiate Dictionary* describes *courage* as "mental or moral strength to venture, persevere, and withstand danger, fear, or difficulty.

These are precisely the qualities needed to be a manager. These are also, I might add, the main qualities needed to get and stay married.

Good managers can never afford to subject themselves, nor their team, to an emotional roller coaster by wearing their heart on their sleeve. They must possess a courageous attitude impervious to the ups and downs of business life. Of course, the wonderful thing about courage is that everyone has the capacity for it. Courage is not borne of a strong body or a well-developed mind; it is a product of the spirit. It's just as likely to be found in an aging grandmother as a Marine Corps sergeant. And it must be evident in a good leader.

Moral Integrity

Integrity is the mystery resource our nation is rediscovering. It seems we had forgotten its importance, or maybe we were hoping it wasn't important at all. But like our forefathers, we have discovered that nothing positive can be established long term without it. I can't help but feel sorry for some of the salespeople and sales managers I occasionally meet; they are hardworking, bright, and ambitious, but noticeably unprincipled. This vacuum of morals and integrity may or may not be their fault, but sooner or later this lack of scruples will likely sabotage their career.

No doubt, one of the most tragic events that can happen to a salesperson or manager is to watch a lifetime of hard work be discounted because of an act of dishonesty in business. To be successful in management, follow this cardinal rule: **Dare to do what's right, fear to do what's wrong, and sacrifice money before principle.** If you can do this without compromise, you'll save yourself a lot of heartache.

Of course managers are responsible for the integrity of their departments. Likewise, they are examples of integrity in their personal lives. Unfortunately, instability in one's home or questionable behavior in one's personal life will also affect performance in business. As a manager, you must command respect in your business and your personal life. This is very difficult to do if you are an alcoholic, a compulsive gambler, or a compulsive skirt- or pants-chaser. These problems very often destroy families and in turn ruin careers.

Tragically, a breakdown in integrity and morals will usually produce what's known in the industry as **sales jumpers** — individuals who hop from job to job, accomplishing little for themselves or the companies that employ them. Such an individual is probably recently divorced, due to an affair or a number of other circumstances, they're usually in poor financial shape, and have recently left a stable, long-term position. Sadly, they now embark on a career of temporary positions that amount to nothing.

To aspire to management is to aspire to principles that esteem moderation, honesty, loyalty, and justice. If you're unfamiliar with these concepts, I can think of no better place to become acquainted with them than that dusty old hidden-away book called the *Bible*. You know the book; it's the one with the first page that reads, "Presented to _____ who is eight years old today, by dear Aunt Edna." It's no secret that many highly successful people have run their businesses and life based on the wisdom contained in its pages. It's also no wonder that almost every book on business and success, from *Poor Richard's Almanac* by Benjamin Franklin to *Think and Grow Rich* by Napoleon Hill, has paraphrased many of the Bible's enduring truths. This book continues to be the world's number-one best-seller year after year, this, despite a history of opposition by repressive governments and intellectual elitists. One final note on integrity, and this is comforting: No one is perfect; mercifully, though, perfection is not required for management — only the desire to try to do what's right.

Motivation

Everyone is motivated to do *something*. I used to hear only about people's lack of motivation, but even the act of doing *nothing* is an act that has been motivated! So the problem isn't really a lack of motivation, but rather too much negative motivation, which results in poor performance. Like everything in life, it's our choice to accept or reject negative motivation — that's what separates the leaders from the followers.

One duty of all managers is to reject the negative motivation of their environment, to act as spark plugs to positively charge and motivate others to accomplish great things. But the plain truth is that not everyone can do that. People fall into two groups: those who can inspire and those who must be inspired, the teachers and the learners. The *type* of motivation that's used is also critical. Anyone can motivate through fear and intimidation. That's not leadership; that's "have-to" management, and "have-to" management is costly and produces only short-term benefits. The best kind of management is **want-to management,** which is fostered by a leader who motivates individuals to perform a task because they *want* to do it, seeing the benefits for themselves and their team. This takes skill, because as individuals each of us is motivated by different needs and wants. Therefore, anyone seeking a management position must be able to identify people's needs and motivate them on an individual basis. Napoleon said it the best: **"A leader is a dealer in hope!"**

WILL MANAGEMENT BE WORTH IT?

If you feel you have the qualities and the desire to pursue a career in management, the next point to consider is, will management be worth it? This is a serious question, and the answer depends on a number of factors, most important of which is how well management is treated by a particular company. You should be prepared to study thoroughly how a company deals with its frontline managers. Companies can then be categorized into poor management environments to work in or good ones. If your present company contributes a poor management environment, it may be prudent to stick to your sales position or, if acquiring a management position, do so for the experience and plan on a speedy departure. The following section outlines some of the telltale signs of a poor management environment.

High Turnover

In some companies a promotion to management is tantamount to a death sentence; even the governor won't be able to deliver a stay of execution. To avoid this, never ignore the turnover rate of managers in a company. There are companies out there that firmly believe that if there's a problem, the answer is always to fire the manager. If you're in management, this type of thinking is hardly conducive to a healthy ego or bank account or a stress-free work life. Don't be misled by the mere offer of management. Always look at the track record, because when you get to the top of the ladder, you'd better be sure you can stay there awhile. The only alternative is to go back down or be pushed off.

To illustrate this, let me relay a story. I have a good friend who was the toast of the company we were selling for, so he eventually was promoted into management. Boy, did we envy him. (I even considered wearing make-up so the green in my face wouldn't show through!) Of course, elated, he bought a new home and wardrobe, and all his family and friends applauded his newfound success. Everyone knew he had "arrived." Then one Friday, after only eight months in his new position, he got the ax. It wasn't really clear why, because his performance seemed more than adequate. Our sales were posting a healthy gain and morale was good. Still, he was let go.

But my friend *should* have expected this type of action. Had he looked more closely at the turnover rate in this position, he would have realized that the odds of long-term employment were definitely against him. He then could have been more cautious and taken steps to protect himself. The point is, unless you can parlay your management position quickly to another company, you should look only for a very stable management environment. Try to find a company where you can expect at least four or five years in management, one that is willing to let you learn in your new position. Remember, it's good to get to the top, but it's better to stay there!

Title-itis

Another dead giveaway of a poor management environment is the onset of the dreaded disease title-itis. Title-itis happens when a person is promoted to a management position but there's no collateral money or influence attached to the promotion. It's sort of like dreaming you've won the lottery; it's nice, but then you wake up. Title-itis is common in those industries where you find legions of vice presidents who own keys to the executive washroom. Their title sounds impressive, but that's about all it amounts to.

More than one salesperson has been bitterly disappointed after moving into management because they suddenly learn they will be earning substantially less in their new position. Still they're expected to work even longer hours. Of course, it's not unusual for some salespeople to earn more than their immediate managers. On the other hand, if sales managers have done a great job improving the performance of their department by showing a substantial profit, they should be adequately compensated. **Management should never be defined by the words** *more hours for less money.* So if you have to moonlight at the local Burger Boy restaurant after your promotion, consider yourself as having been had.

While we are hovering over the subject of title-itis, let's consider that great hybrid management position offered to some salespeople: the selling manager. This is the equivalent of the playing coach and it can sometimes work in a good management environment. Generally, though, it's better to avoid this setup, because it requires you to perform two totally different functions, selling and the managing of salespeople. All too often this becomes a confusing position of conflicting priorities in which the individual ends up performing neither task very well.

The sensible salesperson realizes that a title is only as good as the company behind it and in no way guarantees success. You should first carefully look at the benefits attached to any position offered.

Of course, in a good management environment, the pitfalls previously described don't occur. In such companies, there's a certain stability to a management position. It's nothing like being appointed to the Court for life, but it is a position you can count on for more than six months if you show a reasonable performance. These companies display a real desire to let the novice manager mature and season. Also in a good management environment, a promotion is really a promotion and it includes appropriate compensation and power.

Quality of Life—The Final Frontier

Ultimately, the biggest consideration to be made when chasing the management carrot deals with your quality of life. True, management can bring money and prestige, and that's great, but only if you're happy enough to enjoy them. It's essential to realize that a commitment to a management role is often accompanied by a real change in lifestyle. Take, for example, the carefree salesperson who left the office every day to call on outside clients. Suddenly he may find himself confined to a desk. Many new managers describe this as a very rough adjustment, which some never get over. It's like being a fighter pilot who is suddenly promoted to operations officer; it's very hard to watch the squadron take off into the wild blue yonder while you have to stay behind on the runway.

Moreover, in management it's quite common to have extra demands placed on your time, with more being spent at work and less at home with the family. So before you change jobs, you should consider the experiences of current and previous managers in your company. Are they happy? Are they healthy? Are their families flourishing? Do you really want to be like them, or are you being blinded by the pursuit of the title? Chasing the management carrot is something we are all confronted with. But make sure you think it through, weighing the pros and cons and discovering your capabilities and liabilities.

It's like Clint Eastwood said, "You've got to know your limitations." You also have to know your likes and dislikes. Finally, scout the territory, become familiar with the duties, and true meaning of management. If you do this and management is still for you, good luck! But if it's not, don't become miserable chasing a title for a title's sake. Be true to yourself. It's a wise salesperson who understands the implications of management and why he or she may or may not desire this position.

EXERCISE

Thoroughly and honestly assess your strengths and weaknesses. If your company has a personnel department, ask if you can be tested to determine your management potential. Although by no means the final word, if the test does come out positive you'll feel a lot better. If you can't find a test, write or call my office (address in the back) for an information list.

14

BONUS PLANS
AND SECURITY:
THE PAY AND THE STAY

There is no security on this earth, only opportunity.
DOUGLAS MACARTHUR

English composer William Vaughn once observed, *"If you want to stand in the shortest line in the world, fall in behind those who think they're overpaid."* Today most companies pay their sales staff a combination of salary and bonus. The salary, of course, is straightforward, but the bonus part can be confusing. To shed some light on this, let's look at the purpose and use of the bonus plan.

Years ago most salespeople were paid on straight commission only. Salespeople then were a more independent lot, working as self-employed contractors and paying all their own expenses. This can be very lucrative, and a super salesperson will probably earn more under this system than any other. This is not for the weak at heart, however. There's no safety net and excuses don't count. You're totally on your own. Naturally, because of this, the straight-commission pay system has exacted an extremely high toll in terms of turnover.

This was not only a problem for salespeople, but also for the companies seeking to build and maintain a professional sales staff. They had to spend most of their time recruiting and training new salespeople to replace those leaving. You can still see this operation at work today in some direct-sales companies that market products like vacuum cleaners and encyclopedias.

These operations actually incorporate the high turn-over rate as part of their overall marketing plan. They hire prospects full time and get them to sell to the people they know, fully anticipating some to quit when they finally run out of relatives and friends. By this time the company has already found another candidate ready to do the same. They keep coming and going.

BONUS PLANS

For any company that didn't want to engage in the traditional type of high-turnover operation, the answer was to use the part-time employee or a salary-plus-bonus system. Under such a system, stability could now be introduced into selling by offering people guarantees. This was good for many salespeople and benefitted the companies in the long run.

With this system, companies had an easier time attracting and keeping a quality staff, and there was less energy wasted on constant training. Companies also gained new control over their sales force. They could now make production requirements and expect, within reason, a certain type of conduct from their staff. Of course, this is harder to do when salespeople are on straight commission, because they are basically working for themselves.

Also with such a compensation plan, companies could not be held hostage by one large independent sales

contractor, who could leave and take all his customers
with him. Instead of one big commission earner, the company could employ three smaller, salary-plus-bonus earners.
This gave the companies a new sense of security and continuity in their marketing endeavors.

Without a doubt, the salary-plus-bonus plan has been
extremely successful in adding stability to the profession
of selling. The guarantees now offered by companies
have helped attract numbers of high-quality individuals
to the field of selling.

Of course, you should never forget when considering
the value of guarantees that for everything a company
gives you, they must also take something away. There's
always a balance, and you can lose some independence in
the salary-plus-bonus system. You also may experience a
much more predictable earnings agenda. True, you now
have a guaranteed base salary under you, which is a safety
net, but if you look up you'll probably see a ceiling, which
will limit the amount you can earn.

This is because in most sales operations today, the
purpose of bonus plans is not to pay you a bonanza, but
merely to keep you working at a maximum rate. This is so
you won't degenerate because of the guaranteed salary.
Of course, if you're associated with a company that will
pay you a bonanza and the sky's the limit, count yourself
blessed.

The following section delineates some pivotal points
which will help you to negotiate with bonus plans in
the future.

Bonus Plans Will Change

Bonus plans can be complicated and are continually
changed to satisfy the current needs of management. So
be aware that the rules of the game will be constantly

changing. One year a certain product or feature may provide a high profit margin for the company; in such a case,
you can bet that the bonus plan will be centered around
selling this. Next year, it may be something different and,
sure enough, the bonus plan will reflect that difference.

The other truth about bonus plans is that most companies like to have a predictable payout. So if a bonus
plan is maxed out by the sales force and affords too large
of a payout, it will be changed. This isn't all bad, because
if a bonus plan is not successful and pays a poor compensation, it too will be changed. Remember, companies love
to budget and they love stability, so if a particular plan
doesn't foster this, it will be replaced by one that does.

Needless to say, the companies of today are highly
organized and don't care for big surprises. **So bonus
plans must generate predictable outcomes,** which will
result in profits for the owners and shareholders. In
order to regulate the payout of bonuses, companies can
take any of three approaches:

1. Raise or lower quotas.
2. Pay more or less for the work achieved.
3. Split a territory.

The first two points are self-explanatory, but the third is a
common but a little-understood practice. Splitting a territory works like this: First you take the number of accounts
from which a salesperson is generating business. You then
split this number in half or thirds and assign two or three
people to work these sections. Then a higher amount of
production is required from each section, maximizing
total output. Don't be shocked if all three methods of
bonus regulating are employed during your career; this is
commonplace and you can expect it. Woefully, I've seen
some salespeople never recover from a bonus change,
especially a territory split. They felt betrayed. But, like it or
not, it all comes with the territory!

How to Use Bonus Plans

For some reason, a lot of people have developed a Polly-anna view that their company will do everything it can to pay them unlimited amounts of money in bonuses. Then they are shocked and hurt when a bonus plan doesn't deliver the pot of gold at the end of the rainbow. Again, the truth is that most bonus plans are not there to make you wealthy, but merely to provide incentive to keep you working at capacity. In fact, occasionally you'll find some bonuses are merely part of your overall salary. So, your income may be pretty much the same year to year, regardless of how the bonus plan is changed. Of course, if there's a downturn in the economy, the first cutback may be the bonus plan. That's why it's called a *bonus* and not a guarantee.

I'm not saying there aren't companies out there with fantastic bonus plans, because there are, and if you're selling for one of these, stay there! What I am saying is that most industries behave about the same regarding bonuses. **Bonuses are vital productivity insurance.**

So, with this in mind, what's the best way to use a bonus plan? The first thing to do is to view a bonus as just that—a bonus. You should always resist the temptation to use it for living expenses. It's a far better practice to live on your salary and keep your bonus totally separate. This way you won't have become dependent on your bonus if things go wrong. Unfortunately, many salespeople not only live on their bonuses, they also have them spent well in advance of receiving them. This is living too close to the edge with no margin of safety.

In contrast, the best way to use your bonus is to save as much of it as possible. Granted, you won't become rich overnight from this strategy, but by saving and investing your bonus consistently over time, you will eventually become financially independent. This is a proven way to build wealth, and once you've accomplished this, you'll be immune to the inevitable changes all bonus plans go through. Plus, you'll never again lose sleep just because your bonus might be 10 percent smaller this year.

Job Security

If you ask the average individual today what job security means to them, most would say it's the comfort of knowing they can work for a company as long as they like and their position would never be endangered. So with that definition in mind, I think it is safe to say job security no longer exists on this planet.

Let's face it, today's multinational business world is competitive and changing too rapidly; it's virtually impossible to ensure that *anyone's* position will be around tomorrow. Truly, there are few businesses and opportunities oblivious to these current pressures. If you think you've found a company that offers you real job security, however, then more power to you. On the other hand, if you're part of the norm and are feeling a little anxious, take heart, there may not be job security, but there's definitely *skill security.*

Skill Security

Selling is a skill. A transferable skill. So as long as there are products and services to be purchased, the skill of selling them will always be in demand. Even when the day comes that these products or services become outdated and replaced by new ideas, these new ideas will need to be marketed. To quote the inventor Charles F. Kettering, **"So long as new ideas are created, sales will continue to reach new highs."**

Today many automobile assembly workers have lost their jobs due to automation and competition. In the

United States, an increasing number of cars are being made by robots in foreign plants. Yet there are now more salespeople selling cars than ever before. That's because manufacturing on the assembly line is strictly a mechanical process, a process, some aspects of which barely need human hands.

Selling, however, is an emotional process built on human relationships, and the operative word here is *human*.

You may ask, "Couldn't selling go the same way? Couldn't selling be replaced by some mechanical means?" It's true that a certain amount of selling can be done through mail-order, television, radio, and electronic means. But most of the time this is only used for small-ticket items. When applied to higher-priced commodities, these media are used simply to create name recognition. No, the situations involved in selling are different than in manufacturing. Selling relies upon highly sophisticated two-way communication, and the applications are much too varied to be entrusted to a canned electronic presentation.

The salesperson will always remain vital to the selling process. This was learned the hard way by an insurance company which, a few years back, came up with the brilliant idea to equip each of its salespeople with a videotaped presentation. This video was made by a professional actor who gave a very convincing and all-encompassing presentation. In fact, the presentation was absolutely perfect. Now all that the salesperson had to do was arrive at the prospective buyer's home, sit back, and view this perfect presentation with the client.

Of course, the company's expectations were high. How could it fail? This video would never get tired. It would never forget anything. It would never call in sick. It would give the perfect presentation every time, anytime, and all the time. The only problem, which the company was to find later after sales dropped off the edge of the earth, was that **people didn't want perfect presentations.** What they wanted were imperfect salespeople who could listen to their side of things and with whom they could build a relationship.

Selling is an emotional exchange. The video presentation could give emotion but couldn't receive emotion, and because of this it failed. So until corporate America can find a way to fully duplicate the persuasive wonders of the human being, the skill of selling is forever safe. And therein lies the real job security. Of course, if you're currently employed with a company or selling a certain product line, you've still got to be concerned with maintaining your current position. So here's how to help keep what you've got.

Productivity

Productivity equals security. No matter what situation you're in right now, if you're not growing, you're dying. True security is guaranteed only by being productive. No company or employee can survive if they ever become unprofitable. It's a harsh reality, but in the business world it's the way things work. It's the corporate law of the jungle. To make sure you survive, you've got to always strive to improve.

Perhaps one of the biggest inhibitors to any salesperson's or sales manager's career is to stop doing the things that made them successful. This is so easy to do and is guaranteed to eventually end your career. As Arnold Schwarzenegger says, **"You've got to stay hungry. When you sit down, you go down."**

All work, no matter what kind it is, boils down to repetition and monotony. That's why they call it work! But the truly successful, in spite of this, have the ability to stay excited and motivated about what they're doing. It's not that they're excited about the monotony, the strain, or the repetitiveness; it's just that they keep focused on the eventual reward. They hold this goal in front of them which, in the final analysis, makes the journey as pleasant as the destination.

Earl Nightingale, the motivational thinker and commentator, said it best; to paraphrase: *"Life is funny. You do too much and it can drive you crazy. And yet, if you do too little, you'll simply rust and die."* There has got to be balance, a balance that fosters productivity, which, in itself, will ensure security. After all, security is not a company's or a product's responsibility; it comes from you and you alone. It's your decision, based on how productive you become.

Adaptability

As I stated before, companies and products come and go, but the skill of selling remains. You simply adapt your present selling skill to new concepts, products, and environments. The trick to being adaptable in anything is to be willing to try. Naturally, being willing to try something different would seem a small challenge; however, the willingness to try new things is very difficult for some salespeople because it can often expose you to the risk of failure. Of course, most of us have a strong aversion to failure and seek to avoid it at all costs. We like to seek a comfort zone, a place where we're not challenged above our ability and where we never look foolish. The real winners are those individuals who constantly learn new things, which brings me to another valid point, that earners stay learners.

Selling is not a learned skill in that you are constantly learning. Show me a person in sales who feels he has learned it all, and I'll show you a salesperson with no future. Perhaps you've seen these sagelike individuals. I remember them all too well. I'd see them at sales meetings and seminars. These know-it-all veterans would sit in the back row and make comments under their breath, such as, "That'll never work" or "This guy doesn't know what he's talking about" or "I'll be darned if I'm going to do that."

In virtually every instance where I observed this type of behavior, I noticed that it wasn't long before these salespeople became the least productive and most expendable people on the sales staff. The veteran who stops learning immediately starts to lose his current skills. To compound the problem, the sales world keeps changing, so every year they become less effective. They may lose only 5 percent a year, but soon they can't compete. The extraordinary salespeople, on the other hand, view learning as the means of their security and attack it with excitement and vigor. They'll remain coachable and pliable to new ideas and concepts.

Another principle in staying adaptable is to let go of the past. Make a habit of not using the expression "the good ol' days." Instead, talk of the present or the future. The past is gone and there's nothing you can do about it. You're living in the present and what you do now will affect your future. Some salespeople persist in using phrases like, "We used to do things like this" or "I remember when the company did it this way" or "I used to talk to my client like this." Well, "used to" is nice, but Henry Ford made a great car when he made the Model-T, and there used to be lots of folks driving them. But I don't think you'll see Ford Motor Company bringing back the Model-T this year. What used to be is nice, but it isn't always relevant today.

Always keep looking ahead, and if you find that difficult to do, at least live in the present. The salesperson who can stay open-minded and focused on the future will be constantly building security into his or her career.

Networking

As discussed in Chapter 11 on investing, no market is entirely good or bad. Rather, it's selectively good or bad.

This means that in any particular economic climate, some companies are having explosive growth while other sectors may not be. For instance, real estate may be all the rage this year, whereas oil prices are down. Next year, real estate may be flat, but gold may be soaring. There's a good application to selling in all of this: Certain products and companies may be in a down cycle at the present time, but simultaneously other companies and products are booming.

Of course, the problem is knowing where the opportunities are and how to secure them. I am by no means suggesting that salespeople hop around from product to product or company to company every time there is a downturn. What I am saying is that sometimes a company or product may become obsolete during your career, and if that happens, you'll need to know where the new selling opportunities lie and how to secure them.

To achieve this, one of the best tactics is the use of networking. This can improve your current productivity and ensure career security. Networking is building a chain of related or unrelated business and social contacts who have agreed to help one another. It's the old "you scratch my back and I'll scratch yours" arrangement. As an example, a stockbroker in learning about a particular person's financial situation may suggest this person contact a certain lawyer to have all his wills or other legal work done. In return for this favor, when the lawyer comes into contact with people who need financial advice, she will reciprocate, referring them to the stockbroker.

Why would networking be important to career security in selling? For this reason: The majority of good sales jobs and opportunities are not filled through employment agencies and general advertisements; the best positions are usually offered to people through personal contacts or references. The point is, if you've developed a large network of related and unrelated business contacts, many times you will be privy to information regarding good business opportunities even before this information hits the streets. And if you have provided excellent service and have a good reputation among your networking partners, you will already qualify as a candidate to be sought after by businesses and individuals seeking professional salespeople and managers.

In conclusion, let's highlight the main points to consider about job security:

- There is no job security in selling, but there *is* skill security.
- **Productivity = Security.** The more productive you are, the more indispensable you become, and ultimately the more secure you will be.
- **Adaptability.** To ensure your success and security, you must make sure that you never become obsolete. You've got to be open to new ideas and never stop learning.
- **Networking.** The best opportunities are seldom offered to the public. It therefore pays to develop a large network of contacts and associates who know and respect your work.

EXERCISES

A. Immediately set up a separate networking file.

B. Separate and save your bonus! Don't live on it!

C. Keep current on all information regarding selling and your industry. This means attending meetings and conferences, regardless of how much you know. Remember: **The meeting you miss is the meeting you need.**

15

JOB AND CAREER MOVES: CROSSROADS OF OPPORTUNITY

The world makes way for the person
who knows where they're going.
RALPH WALDO EMERSON

The grass is always greener on the other side, but don't forget, it's just as hard to mow. Such is the single greatest piece of advice ever given to those contemplating change in their life. Then there is William Shakespeare, who wrote (to paraphrase), "There comes to each life a high tide of opportunity, and if one will seize it, they will be carried to prosperity. However, once this tide is gone, it is forever lost." One statement is a strong proponent for change; the other a caution against it. It's against this conflicting backdrop that we will deal with the exciting subject of changing jobs and careers.

I think you'll agree that the days of lifelong employment at one company are probably gone. This is old news to people in sales and management, who traditionally have a higher turnover rate in the business world. In jest, in some companies you are considered a veteran if you carry business cards with your name preprinted! So, people in sales can probably expect to make a few job changes during their career. Some will be involuntary company closings, relocations, and things you can't control. Most other changes, however, will be instigated by you. These voluntary moves will represent the most important decisions in your career and can single-handedly determine your overall success.

CONTEMPLATING A CHANGE?

It's not just a matter of how good you are in sales or in management, you also have to be in the right vehicle. In today's Grand Prix racing, even the greatest driver in the world is guaranteed to lose if he's driving the family car. In sales as in racing, the vehicle is as important as the driver. There may come a time when you'll want to, or have to, choose a new vehicle in order to win. To help you in this decision-making process, here are some principles to consider when contemplating a job or business change.

Never Trade a Good Deal for a Good Deal

You see this blunder made all the time. It goes like this: A salesperson in a stable, well-paying job gets an offer from a distributor, client, or competitor. The offer is, of course, for more money. So without much thought, the salesperson accepts the new position. Six months later they're no better off and they realize they've gained nothing. Now they're miserable. In such a situation, no one wins; the original employer is out the cost of training, the salesperson is disillusioned, and the new employer has an unhappy employee. This all could have been avoided if the salesperson had analyzed the true worth of the original position and weighed it against the new offer. Salary is only part of the story. What about security? What about the net worth of your present benefit package, including medical, dental, stock purchases, retirement plans, company car, and expense accounts? What about the possible cost of a move? And how about the strength and position of your new product in the marketplace? Finally, how about seniority? Make sure you evaluate all of this before you consider any move. If you do this and your offer still nets you an increase of 25 percent or more and it looks secure . . . you may seriously want to consider it. However, most of the time after careful analysis you'll probably find you don't need a change as much as you need to stay put, manage your money better, and work harder. Don't get caught trading a good deal for a good deal.

Never Make a Major Decision When You're Down

If you are considering a change, before you do anything try to discover the true motive behind your desire. Is it because a real opportunity has presented itself which will allow you to advance in your career? Or are you thinking of changing only because you came in second in the latest sales contest and your ego is hurting? The fact is, many people make major decisions at the wrong time, usually when they're on an emotional low. They also make major decisions for the wrong reasons. Many times they don't decide to leave a job for a better opportunity so much as to get away from a set of unresolved problems. This is, of course, the easy way out, but it's also the wrong way.

Everybody is down from time to time, and problems from boredom or personal conflict are all part of your business life. But most problems can be resolved. So don't let temporary difficulties dictate your final decision to leave a position. If you're considering a change, try to make your decisions in the proper frame of mind and with the right motive. Take your time and don't act impulsively. A good question to ask yourself is: Am I running to something or am I running away from something?

Be Choosy

After careful consideration, if you still feel you want to make a change, take a tip from the acting world. In the film industry, actors loathe being typecast, so it's not surprising how choosy they become when they have the opportunity to pick their next role. In the sales business, though, it's astonishing how many people unwittingly typecast themselves by choosing the same old lines of selling, the same strata of income, and the same positions. **If you're going to change, don't limit your options by past achievements.** As the poet Robert Browning states, "It's the looking downward that makes one dizzy." So look higher and think bigger. And remember the following sobering story.

There was once a successful salesperson who was earning more than $100,000 a year. He had the opportunity to meet an associate in selling who was a million-dollar-a-year earner. After all the polite chitchat was over, the big question was finally asked: "Why do you earn a million dollars a year and I make only $100,000?" With no delay, the seven-figure earner looked the six-figure earner straight in the eye and said with a smile, "Because that's all you wanted."

What do *you* want? Whatever it is, be choosy. Never sell yourself short. Why not go for it? A change is a chance. So start your quest at the top. You can always work down, if need be.

Trust — But Verify

The phrase *trust but verify* originated during Ronald Reagan's presidential administration. It's excellent advice, not only for politicians but for salespeople as well. When you're employed, it appears as though there are unlimited options available to you in the marketplace; it's only when you seriously start looking and trying to pin them down that you realize that not everything is as it appears. For instance, take that competitor who for years has been telling you if you ever need a job, don't hesitate to call him first. When put to the test, however, he informs you they don't have an opening at this time, but call back in six months. The fact is, you are never in a better position of strength and bargaining power than when you are currently employed.

So don't be fooled. This reminds me of the paradox I faced many times in my younger days while dating. It seemed when I was out on a date, there was always an abundance of eligible prospects; but if I ever dared to venture out unaccompanied to the same places, many of these prospects seemed to vanish mysteriously. The ones who were left appeared far less interested than I had originally thought. The moral of the story is, if you are considering a change, first trust, then verify that you have a sound offer to go to. This seems like common sense, but you'd be surprised how many salespeople and managers find themselves with nowhere to go, because they trusted a verbal promise of employment made six months earlier. You've got to know for certain that the company and opportunity you're considering has the ability and desire to deliver what it promised.

Always do a complete background study on your new opportunity. Discreetly talk to as many current and former employees as possible, checking their satisfaction level and confidence in the company. Also make sure you come to a complete understanding of your new duties and exactly what will be expected of you. Above all, trust but verify that you have a sound offer. There are few things more unpleasant than leaving a sure thing for nothing.

Get It in Writing

Recently while playing tennis (that's what I do when I'm disgusted with golf), I heard a story that had a familiar ring to it. My tennis partner, also a salesperson, was relating to me how he had become disenchanted with the company he was currently selling for. Apparently he had approached his manager and told him of his concerns and that he was considering leaving. Of course, that got the sales manager's attention because my friend was a real workhorse for the company. So the manager suggested they talk it over. During the conversation the manager proposed that my friend be promoted to management, thus becoming eligible for 5 percent of the profits from his department. Needless to say, this completely changed my friend's attitude from disenchantment to excitement and hopefulness. Of course, I immediately congratulated my friend and inquired when this change would take place. It was then that I noticed his facial expression become quite tense. He said, "Well, due to an economic downturn, my manager said it wouldn't be a good time to institute this change now, but possibly in six months to a year."

I think you can tell I'm not a pessimist; I wouldn't even consider myself a realist. I'm a bona fide optimist. But, when I heard my friend's story, I found very little to be optimistic about. In fact, I would consider this is a big disappointment waiting to happen. I base my supposition on a multitude of similar stories from salespeople who have been promised things or thought they were promised things only to have them never come to pass.

Most salespeople realize that some business associates make promises merely to attract and keep good salespeople. What many salespeople fail to understand, though, is that these promises are conditional, verbal, and not freestanding. Most of the time such promises are made in goodwill, but they are usually contingent upon the salesperson or manager radically improving the growth of the company.

Of course, what a salesperson or sales manager perceives as good growth may not necessarily reflect management's view. It seems the big problem is that both parties, sales and management, hear only what they want to during the recruiting or negotiating process, laying the groundwork for future misunderstanding, confusion, and bitterness. That's why **having an agreement on paper** is the only means to alleviating this problem! This protects both you and the company. After all, if a company or business associate is really serious about offering you a pay raise, partnership, or management position, they should be willing to back it up in writing. Of course, it takes a lot of brass to ask for a written agreement, but remember, all they can do is say no. And it's better for you to know up front how serious they are about fulfilling their promises, rather than being surprised, powerless, and bitter down the road. So get it in writing and sell this idea by showing all parties concerned how this will benefit and protect them in the future.

Leave on Good Terms

Upon receiving the customary two-week notice of an employee leaving, some companies request that the employee leave even sooner. The reason is that from experience companies know some departing employees can be extremely disruptive. After all, many employees now feel they have absolutely nothing to lose and so may use their remaining time to settle old scores and vent past frustrations against individuals and company alike. It's like a messy divorce. Unfortunately, the employee who chooses this course of behavior may be inflicting injury only upon himself. The right move is to never burn your bridges.

This is the time to bolster friendships and leave on the best terms possible.

You've probably heard the story of the Spanish explorer Cortez who upon reaching the New World immediately burned his ships. Now he and his men would have but one option — to go forward. This was a brilliant and successful strategy for Cortez; in the business world, however, it's not recommended. Having only the option of going forward is extremely impractical. For one thing, it really is a small world and you never know when your paths may cross again with a former company owner, manager, or associate. The business world is not static, and past relationships have an uncanny way of turning up in new business arrangements.

Another reason to leave on good terms is to allow yourself the privilege of using your past employer's influence through references. Many times in my own career I have been aided by the influence or good word of a former employer or business partner. References are a valuable asset to have on your side, so never underestimate their worth.

The final reason for leaving on good terms is an extremely practical one: You never know when you might want your old job back. I know everybody says they'll never go back, but, you don't know what circumstances you'll be faced with in the future. And you may find the business opportunity that looked so bright wasn't nearly as good as you thought it would be.

I used to be under the impression that once a person left a company there would be no way that company would hire them back again. But through experience I know that this isn't true. In fact, I have many friends who have left companies or business relationships to pursue other ventures and have come back, happily, I might add, to work for past employers. This option was made available to them only because as prudent salespeople they made every effort to leave on good terms. Forget the fantasies of giving the boss a piece of your mind when you leave. **Remember, if you tell your boss what you really think of him or her, the truth will set you free, indefinitely.**

Finally, job and career changes, if executed properly, can be some of the most profitable and exciting events in our lives. This is especially true when we put ourselves in firm control of the decision-making process and diligently seek to avoid the pitfalls associated with such a change.

EXERCISES

A. To keep career moves from being triggered by the wrong reasons, practice daily Benjamin Franklin's advice, *"Write your injuries in dust, your benefits in marble."*

B. THINK, THINK AGAIN!

16

SLUMPS AND BUMPS ON THE ROAD TO WINNING

Only the mediocre are always at their best.
SOMERSET MAUGHAM

They say no sailor ever became great on a calm sea. I know that's true, but when you're the sailor and the boat's rocking plus you're turning three shades of green, it's hard to be so philosophical.

Everybody loves to talk about successful people. We are quick to admire their accomplishments, but few people study to see the struggles and setbacks that go on behind the scenes in a winner's life. That's a shame, because if your performance should suddenly falter or go into an extended slump, you'll need to know how to diagnose and fix the problem fast. So let's skip the ups, just for a moment, and look at the possible bumps and slumps you might experience on the road to winning.

MOMENTUM—THE BIG MO

There I was, competing in my first sales contest for a trip to Hawaii. My wife and I were so excited we could hardly stand it. After all, the last trip we made was a pilgrimage to Wiggins, Mississippi, to watch our relatives fight at a family picnic. Anyway, I worked hard and when the results finally came in, we came up winners! So it was off to the islands for two weeks, and everything was coming up macadamia nuts!

When we got back, I traded in my tan for a business suit and went back to work. I was really fired up and was determined to make more appointments and close more sales than ever before. I was ready to set the world ablaze. The only problem was that after a week back on the job, nothing was happening. At first I wasn't too worried, because I knew that next week things would get better. But they didn't. Everything had come to a screeching halt. It was then that I made a call of desperation to my national sales director and frantically explained to him what was happening, or should I say *not* happening.

He listened very intently and then calmly said, "Don't worry about it, you just lost the big Mo."

I said, "The big Mo, what's that?"

He said, "You've lost your momentum."

I then responded, "That's comforting to know, but for heaven's sake, tell me how to get it back!"

So here, with some other good advice, is what I learned.

Re-Goal

Probably the most dangerous time in a salesperson's career is when they have experienced a major victory. Maybe they've just gotten a promotion or received an unusually large bonus. Or, like myself, won a hard-fought sales contest. **Whatever the pinnacle achieved, the real trick is to leave the mountaintop as soon as possible.** Certainly you can enjoy your accomplishments, but you've got to resist the temptation to stay in the present or the past. You must quickly climb down again and set your sights on another peak.

To keep momentum going, immediately replace vanquished goals with new ones, because without a new goal your performance will slowly drift into mediocrity. You must have something to fight for at all times. This, in itself, will help renew your energy and keep your performance sharp. In industry, to remain competitive companies must re-tool. The same principle applies to sales. Sensible salespeople set goals and use them as tools to build momentum to keep up to speed for the next victory.

Goal Setting — In a Nutshell

Ultimately, to set your goals you should first find a purpose. A purpose is larger than a goal because it's your reason for living. At its best, a purpose can be eternal. Safe to say those who find a purpose in life rarely suffer from burnout or boredom. In goal setting, it is advisable to always have two goals. One should be long term, ten years or more, and the other short term. The long-term goal should be big — as big as possible — yet still attainable and in line with your purpose. This should be made with the idea that your reach should exceed your grasp. The short-term goal, although harmonious with the overall objective, should consist of smaller steps. These are goals to be achieved on a monthly, weekly, and daily basis. Write down your daily goals at the beginning or end of each day — the six most important things you must accomplish in your business and personal life. Regardless of all else, get these things done. This is a time-honored technique that has worked well for many business, military, and political leaders over the years. It's simple and effective. Short-term goals will serve as your compass, keeping you on track toward your final objective. Use a good daily planner to document all this in one place.

Of course, you'll always hear that the secret to goal setting is to first write them down. This is true, but only to a point. I've met and spoken to thousands of sales and businesspeople, and most write their goals down. Some of them write beautifully, detailing step-by-step. Others simply have magazine pictures plastered on their refrigerators depicting objects they desire, such as homes, cars, or slim bodies. The truth is, few from either group attain these goals. Yet I have known champions who have reached their goals without ever writing them down. Why? Because writing down a goal doesn't work unless you passionately need to reach it. For some, this passion can transcend the need for paper and ink. The great basketball coach, Pat Riley, gave us the true key to goal setting when he said, **"You've got to want something so bad it hurts."** In my mind, the very best portrait of the passion needed to accomplish any worthwhile goal is portrayed by actress Vivian Leigh in *Gone with the Wind* when she stands silhouetted against the sky and declares, "as God is my witness, I'll never be hungry again." Is there any doubt in your mind that she means business? I call this the "Scarlett O'Hara test." So by all means, write down your goals, but first, like Scarlett O'Hara, make sure you have the passion necessary to achieve them. Along these same lines, some time ago Harvard Professor William James wrote these pertinent words: "In almost any subject your passion for the subject will save you. If you care enough for a result, you most certainly will attain it."

Accelerate Your Activity

Any discussion of lost momentum involves a look at the relationship of energy expended to momentum acquired. Simply put, it takes a lot more energy to build momentum than it does to keep it. For example, it requires an extreme concentration of power to get the space shuttle off the ground. Everything is at maximum output. However, upon breaking through the atmosphere, the astronaut has the luxury of being able to throttle back, using far less power yet still achieving impressive performance. Creating momentum in selling is a lot like getting the shuttle off the ground. You have to expend a tremendous amount of energy, at first.

In selling, the energy you use is represented by your activity. To create momentum, this activity must be greatly accelerated. Initially, this could be achieved by perhaps doubling the amount of calls and appointments you would normally book in a given time frame. The rule is, **if you compress activity, you'll reap explosive growth.** The same thing applies if momentum starts to wane. The only way to boost it is to increase your activity or energy output.

Many think that great salespeople work at the same level all of the time. That's seldom true. Most work in controlled spurts, which are incredibly intense and take their production and performance to new heights. Once this is achieved, their position can be maintained with less effort and with proper monitoring.

Patience and Pipelines

Of course, sometimes when momentum is lost, it's not our fault. We may have experienced an accident or illness, or possibly our company has fallen victim to a strike, which has killed our business. Whatever the reason, once momentum is lost, you'll need to be patient and not become overly frustrated if things don't turn around overnight. Momentum takes time to build.

Perhaps one of the best ways to illustrate this is the pipeline theory: If you take a long, empty pipeline, you first have to fill that pipeline full before any substantial flow comes out the other end. In starting to build momentum from scratch, the same principle is true; you've got to first totally fill your pipeline with appointments, presentations, and proposals before any results start to show.

The trick is to be patient and keep filling your pipeline, making sure that you concentrate on the *input end* of the pipeline and not the *output end*.

GETTING OUT OF A SLUMP

When you picture someone in a selling slump, you usually think of a period of time when production is low. That's not the true definition of a slump, because all performances have peaks and valleys. The sporting world can offer us an example of this: For instance, did you know that in golf most players win the majority of their prize money for the entire year in only a three-week period? Does that mean they were in a slump the rest of the year? Of course not. All performances are marked by fluctuations.

Like the song says, "When you're hot, you're hot, when you're not, you're not." So what constitutes a slump? Basically what determines a slump is how you view the situation. A real slump is characterized not only by poor performance, but also by a crisis in confidence, where we start to question our own abilities. This doubt usually causes anxiety, self-consciousness, and low morale, which in turn leads to below-average performance. It's a vicious cycle that can go round and round and, sadly, down and down. The question is, How do we break out of this destructive cycle? Here are some suggestions.

Fundamentals — Or Check If It's Plugged In

After coming home from a vacation, I sat down in front of the television eager to watch an old movie. I pressed the remote control and nothing happened. No picture, no nothing. The next thing I knew, I had the remote control torn apart and was searching for one of the rarest commodities known to modern man — the AA battery. As I frantically dug through the kitchen junk drawer, my wife heard me grumbling and asked what was the matter. I told her the television didn't work because something was wrong with the remote control, but not to worry because I was going to fix it. My wife then uttered those words we husbands love to hear: "Did you check to see if the TV is plugged in?"

I said, "It couldn't be that."

It was that. Boy, did I feel stupid.

I could have saved all that time and energy if I had first checked the obvious.

There's a big lesson in this story, relating to the times in selling when nothing is working: Don't forget the fundamentals. Let's use golf again to illustrate this point. Take the immortal Jack Nicklaus, who is considered by many to be the greatest golfer of all time. Although not as active now, Nicklaus probably knows more about golf than anyone. Yet each year before playing the circuit, or whenever his game started to suffer, Nicklaus would spend time with his longtime friend and personal coach, the late Jack Grout. This wise teacher would begin by treating the champion like a mere beginner. He would check Nicklaus on the simplest of fundamentals, like how he held his club and his overall posture. Only after the basics were checked and adjusted, did they go on to explore deeper matters. They knew from experience that in executing the simplest of skills, bad habits and idiosyncrasies can develop, and left unchecked, they can ruin a performance.

Likewise in sales, never overlook the obvious. When your confidence starts to falter because of slumping performance, the first thing to do is go back to the basics. Review the quality of your presentation, your close, objection killing, and so on. **Always check the fundamentals and the obvious first,** the problem is likely there.

Get Help

No one is an island; we all need someone. This is especially true if we're in a sales slump. I mean, why go through all that introspection and self-analysis when you're too close to the situation to see the problem anyway? In doing this, we often end up putting ourselves down and saying negative things like, "What's the matter with me anyway?" and "Maybe I should get a job with the government; at least they don't expect results."

A far better approach would be to ask for the aid of someone you respect, someone trustworthy and experienced in your field. Talk to him or her first about what's happening to you. You'll be surprised at how much better you'll feel by getting your problem out in the open. Also, many times because of their distance from a problem, others have a better perspective and can offer some sound solutions. There's not much new under the sun, and if you have a problem in sales, chances are others have been there before, and what's better, they know the way back.

Remember: The mark of true champions is they're humble enough to admit they don't have all the answers. Interestingly, some people even suggest expanding this idea of seeking help into what they call a brain trust. This is where you build a network of four or five people you can consult for career guidance. There is safety and wisdom in many counselors, so don't go it alone. A burden shared is much easier to carry.

Take a Break

If after you've tried everything to end a slump and failed, the only thing left to do is nothing. That by itself may do the trick. After all, it's no secret that a lot of people report increases in performance levels after a good layoff.

Perhaps this is because the pressure is off and expectations are lower coming back. This leaves you free to perform without thinking too much and worrying about making mistakes. Of course, another reason could be because previously you were mentally and physically exhausted. Whatever the reason, a good layoff can work wonders and it's imperative to realize the need for intervals of inactivity.

For most people a good layoff usually consists of taking the standard two-week vacation once a year. During this time, they usually try to explore the entire continent by car, or travel to stay with innumerable relatives until everybody is neurotic. I fondly remember what our motto used to be, *Hurry up, we're on vacation.* With this attitude, we defeated the whole purpose of time off and generally came back in worse shape than when we left. It may be a better idea to be a little less ambitious on vacations.

We should also learn to rest and rejuvenate on a more frequent basis than just two weeks per year. This may be accomplished by engaging in activities year-round that are unrelated to business. Too many people are one dimensional, focusing only on work. They focus so much that everything else is just a blur. To them, rest and rejuvenation means eight hours of sleep and then back to work. This may meet their physical needs, but much more is needed psychologically.

For instance, the mind has to be periodically engaged with a new set of challenges or it will continue to endlessly process its present information. This eventually leads to boredom and poor performance. To avoid this you should seek out new activities. Also make sure this is something you really enjoy. In keeping with this idea, don't automatically head for the golf course or tennis courts just because everyone in your office plays. Do what you like to do.

Take your example from Malcolm Forbes, the publisher and personality, who loved to ride motorcycles and hot-air balloons, even into his later years. Many other great people have had toy train collections, flower gardens, or woodworking shops. And there is absolutely nothing wrong with resurrecting your twenty-year-old stamp collection. Doing something you like will defend yourself from career burnout or worse. Remember, if you can't find the time for recreation, you're destined to sooner or later find the time for illness. Everyone needs a personalized escape from the pressures of business. To be effective in sales is to be aware of the power of rest and its effects on performance.

Relish the Fight as Much as the Prize

One of the greatest secrets to longevity in any endeavor is to love the act of what you're doing more than the result. If winning becomes an addiction that you must constantly have in order to perform, it can overshadow everything. With this attitude, if winning is not achieved performance can nosedive to unbelievable lows and stay there. But if you love what you're doing even more than the winning, your performance levels will usually be consistent and more resistant to slumps.

One of the best examples of someone who loved what he was doing is the great baseball pitcher, Nolan Ryan. People marvel at the length of Nolan's career. How did he stay competitive for so long? Usually once an athlete reaches a certain age, it's a rapid descent to retirement and the average and ordinary. Some pros have said if they can't be number one anymore, it's just no fun to play. Not so for Nolan Ryan, and therein lies his secret. People like Nolan Ryan don't need the winning nearly as much as they need the joy of competing. This is why they become and stay champions for so long! Even well into his forties Ryan remained a threat to major-league hitters.

I like how German tennis great Boris Becker sees it; he said, **"I love winning, I can take the losing, but most of all I love to play."** I think we can learn a lot from champions in that nothing can improve our performance more than simply falling in love with whatever we're doing and worrying less about what we're achieving.

EPILOGUE

Come then, let us to our task.
WINSTON CHURCHILL

It's been said there are but three places in which a person will spend their life. One is in the midst of a storm, the second is coming out of a storm, and the third is heading into another storm. Not a very comforting philosophy, is it? I think this statement must have been made by the same optimist who said, "Life is hard, then you die." At any rate, I'm sure most of us will experience a ton of sunny days in between. But if things do occasionally get rough and you're facing some bumps and slumps in your career, keep in mind this thought:

These are exactly the moments that teach us how to win. There really is no achievement without adversity. Ultimately your success in life will be measured not by how well you did in the good times, but how you reacted and recovered from the bad ones.

So with this I bid you my favorite old Scottish farewell: **May God bless you to live as long as you want to, and want to as long as you live!**

Color Versus Control

PERSONALITY TEST

Color: The quality that makes an
indistinguishable object noticeable

Control: The ability to regulate and command

What makes a successful person successful? As you can imagine there are many factors involved. Possibly the two strongest traits, however, are one's ability to cultivate individual talents and creativity, and to harness these gifts with discipline and directed energy. In this test a person's creativity and talent are represented by the word *Color.* This Color is what makes you special, what makes you, *you.* On the other hand, the discipline and directed energy are depicted by the word *Control.* This test seeks to give people a general idea of their Color versus Control quotient.

This evaluation is designed for training and education purposes only. The author cannot be held liable for interpretations by others.

To begin the test, simply circle the answer that best describes you. To ensure usefulness, be honest and be true to thyself. Remember, there are no right or wrong answers, and usually your first answer is best.

271

COLOR

Circle one:

1. While waiting in an office or a line, do you strike up a conversation with strangers?

   Never   Seldom   Sometimes   Often   Always

2. Do you really love to meet new people?

   Never   Seldom   Sometimes   Often   Always

3. Do business associates often call you by a nickname?

   Never   Seldom   Sometimes   Often   Always

4. Do you enjoy joining new associations, clubs, and organizations?

   Never   Seldom   Sometimes   Often   Always

5. Do you still play a musical instrument regularly or frequently sing, besides in church?

   Never   Seldom   Sometimes   Often   Always

6. Do you faithfully engage in any classic artistic endeavors such as poetry, sculpture, painting, or creative writing?

   Never   Seldom   Sometimes   Often   Always

7. Do you often tell jokes?

   Never   Seldom   Sometimes   Often   Always

8. Would people say that you are a good dancer?

   Never   Seldom   Sometimes   Often   Always

9. When you leave work do you totally leave it behind?

   Never   Seldom   Sometimes   Often   Always

10. Would people ever say that you have a great sense of humor?

    Never   Seldom   Sometimes   Often   Always

11. Do you dream about being famous?

    Never   Seldom   Sometimes   Often   Always

12. Are you comfortable being the center of attention?

    Never   Seldom   Sometimes   Often   Always

13. Do you feel comfortable being perceived as different from the group that you're with?

    Never   Seldom   Sometimes   Often   Always

14. Have you ever seriously planned to go hang gliding, scuba diving, mountain climbing, car racing, bungee jumping, para sailing, or the like?

    Never   Seldom   Sometimes   Often   Always

15. Do people ever comment on your clothing?

    Never   Seldom   Sometimes   Often   Always

16. Some people are settlers, others are explorers. Would you consider yourself an explorer?

    Never   Seldom   Sometimes   Often   Always

17. Do you still consistently play sports in a league or individually?

    Never   Seldom   Sometimes   Often   Always

18. Without the use of excessive amounts of alcohol, would you consider standing on stage and singing Karaoke?

    Never   Seldom   Sometimes   Often   Always

19. Would people say that you're a good storyteller?

    Never   Seldom   Sometimes   Often   Always

20. Do you like experimenting and finding new ways of doing things?

Never   Seldom   Sometimes   Often   Always

Color total _____

CONTROL

1. Do you make daily to-do lists or use a daily planner?

Never   Seldom   Sometimes   Often   Always

2. Do you save money regularly?

Never   Seldom   Sometimes   Often   Always

3. Some people jump from one interest or task to another, but do you stick to one task until it's properly completed?

Never   Seldom   Sometimes   Often   Always

4. Is your car clean inside and out?

Never   Seldom   Sometimes   Often   Always

5. Is your desk clean and uncluttered?

Never   Seldom   Sometimes   Often   Always

6. Compared with others, do you handle paperwork promptly and accurately?

Never   Seldom   Sometimes   Often   Always

7. Do you always thoroughly read the instructions before starting a task?

Never   Seldom   Sometimes   Often   Always

8. Do you meet most deadlines without leaving things to the last minute?

Never   Seldom   Sometimes   Often   Always

9. Would people describe you as being well organized?

   Never   Seldom   Sometimes   Often   Always

10. Do you plan your vacations early and in specific detail?

   Never   Seldom   Sometimes   Often   Always

Control total _____ (multiply x 2) _____

ACTIVE/RECEPTIVE

1. Do you speak up and freely give your opinion to others besides your family?

   Never   Seldom   Sometimes   Often   Always

2. Is the main goal of sports and recreational games always to win?

   Never   Seldom   Sometimes   Often   Always

3. Would others describe you as a good seller of ideas?

   Never   Seldom   Sometimes   Often   Always

4. Do you want to lead others as opposed to follow?

   Never   Seldom   Sometimes   Often   Always

5. Would people say you're really competitive?

   Never   Seldom   Sometimes   Often   Always

6. When the opportunity presents itself, do you volunteer to lead groups of people seeking to accomplish a task?

   Never   Seldom   Sometimes   Often   Always

7. Would you be vocal and object to a company policy that you didn't agree with, even though everyone else was happy with it?

   Never   Seldom   Sometimes   Often   Always

8. Can you make decisions quickly, not laboring over them?

   Never   Seldom   Sometimes   Often   Always

9. When emotionally hurt, some people hold their feelings in, but do you let your feelings be known right away?

   Never   Seldom   Sometimes   Often   Always

10. If a restaurant serves you food that you feel is not up to quality, do you send it back?

    Never   Seldom   Sometimes   Often   Always

Active/Receptive totals _____ (multiply x 2) _____

Now total up each category of questions by assigning a number value to each answer. For example:

Never = 1   Seldom = 2   Sometimes = 3   Often = 4   Always = 5

Add up total points for Color questions.
Add up total points for Control questions.
Add up total points for Active/Receptive questions.

                    Color total   _____
                    Control total   _____
Assertiveness (Active/Receptive) total   _____

Now plot the totals for each group by placing a dot in the appropriate lettered column at the correct level on the graph provided. Next join all three dots with two straight lines. A to B, and B to C. Please note: A high score can be good in a category, but more important is the relationship of your scores to one another.

A		B		C	
A		B		C	ACTIVE
100		100		100	
90		90		90	
80		80		80	
70		70		70	
60		60		60	
50		50		50	ASSERTIVENESS
40		40		40	
30		30		30	
20		20		20	
10		10		10	
0				0	
A	COLOR	B	CONTROL	C	RECEPTIVE

RESULTS

Your scores will determine to which of the three major categories you belong. The major categories are:

- The Color group, Moderate or Intense
- The Control group, Moderate or Intense
- The Balanced group, Moderate or Intense

In addition there are two other minor divisions to each major category. They are:

- Active
- Receptive

This deals with your assertiveness level, with active being more assertive and receptive being less.

To find your category, read the following steps.

1. First, note which score is higher between your **Color** and **Control** totals, columns A and B on the graph.

2. Next, determine if the **higher** score between the two is at least 15 points more than the lower score.

3. If you find there is at least a 15-point difference, your major category is the **higher** score of the two. So you're either in the **Color** category or **Control** category. **Important:** If there is not at least 15 points difference between your Color and Control scores, you qualify for the **Balanced** category.

For example: If your Color score was 70 and your Control score 50, there is at least 15 points difference, so your major category would be the **Color** group, which is the highest score. But if the scores were reversed, with your Control score being 70 and your Color score being 50, you would fall into the **Control** group.

Finally, if your two scores were within 15 points of each other, you would fall into the **Balanced** group. For instance, if your Control score was 75 and your Color score was 70, there is only a 5-point difference. This puts you in the **Balanced** group. Note which major category you fall into: Color, Control, or Balanced.

4. Next you need to determine if you are Moderate or Intense in your major category description. If your Color and Control scores are both above the 50 percent mark, you are a **Moderate**. However, if at least one score is below 50 percent, you are **Intense**.

5. Now you should know which of the three major categories you fit into and whether you are Moderate or Intense. All that is left is to determine your Assertiveness rating. For this, look at column C on the graph. If you are above the 50 percent mark, you are Active; below the 50 percent mark, you are Receptive. Now you have an extra description to add to your major category profile. For instance, you could be a:

- Color Intense who is Active
- Balanced Moderate who is Receptive
- Control Moderate who is Active

My major group and minor descriptions are:

Major group	Moderate or Intense	Assertiveness
_____	_____	_____

GENERAL DESCRIPTIONS

The Color Group ⑤

To be in the Color category, your Color total must be at least 15 points higher than your Control total. If both your Color and Control scores are above 50 percent, you are a **Color Moderate.** If at least one is below, you are a **Color Intense.** There are also two other divisions in the Color group. They are the Active, with an assertiveness rating above 50 percent, and the Receptive, those whose assertiveness rating is below 50 percent. Most of the information below applies to the entire Color group; there are some differences, however, which will be pointed out.

As a Color group individual, you have a broad variety of interests and natural talent. You're the spice of life. This is especially true the higher your color totals are above the 50 percent mark. At these levels you find you are a quick study and can master new skills easily if you maintain focus. A Color group individual loves change and most often will choose variety over routine. With this you enjoy flexibility and the freedom to move about and set your own schedule. You may be strongly ' attracted to the independence of a selling career.

In decision making you will often base your judgment on the circumstance rather than adhere to set policies and procedures. This is sometimes seen as risky, but can be popular with associates. If you're Active in your Assertiveness total (above 50 percent), you are definitely not shy and you make your presence and ideas quickly known. In addition, you probably possess good persuasive powers and communicate and connect easily with people from all walks of life. If you are Receptive in the Assertiveness score (below 50 percent), the story is much different. Here you are probably more reserved and less willing to express your thoughts and feelings to others. This can allow you to be manipulated, which you oftentimes resent. As an overall Color group individual, your greatest challenges come in the areas of organization, persistence, and attention to detail. In other words, *discipline*. This is especially true when you are Color Intense and there is a wide variance between your Color score and your Control score, with your Control score falling below 50 percent. In this situation you often get good ideas but have difficulty seeing them through. This is because after an idea has been conceived it takes a consistent, detailed effort to make it profitable. In business, this lack of organization can be detrimental to keeping customers long term. In sales you may be a good closer but not much on follow-up. Here you have to work at it.

Another characteristic of the Color Intense is that they often say they work well under pressure, but this is because with poor organizational skills, they've had lots of practice. *Please note, however, if both your Color and Control scores are above 50 percent, you are a Color Moderate, and although you enjoy the benefits of creativity and natural talent, you also have enough discipline and organizational skills to avoid the downsides just discussed.*

In leadership style the Color group will gravitate toward a more democratic approach, giving subordinates a lot of control and power. Again this can be popular with employees, but it must be monitored very closely for positive results. Of course in the lower assertiveness levels found in the Receptive range, you are not likely at present to seek a leadership role. Plus you probably don't find sales to be your favorite habitat.

As a Color group individual you are in the enviable position of significantly increasing your overall performance and success by seeing the value of adding more control and discipline to your life. This is especially true if your **Color Intense** and your Control score is below 50 percent. Again it is less of a concern to a **Color Moderate.** In Assertiveness if you are Receptive, you will benefit not only by striving to become better organized, but also by exercising more will. This is not easy, but with each victory comes tremendous exhilaration. It just takes the realization that you can't please everybody, so go ahead and be yourself—you've got a lot to offer.

In conclusion, the Color group individual should remember that if you possess both talent and discipline, you can accomplish anything you desire.

The Control Group

To be in the Control group your Control rating is at least 15 points higher than your Color score. Plus, if both your Control and Color scores are above 50 percent, you are a **Control Moderate.** If at least one score is below 50 percent, you are a **Control Intense.** There are two other divisions of the Control Group. Those who are Active, with an assertiveness rating above 50 percent, and those who are Receptive, with an assertiveness rating below 50 percent. Most of the information to follow applies to both groups; there are some differences, however, which will be pointed out.

As a Control group individual you are the backbone of the business world. You are the rock, well organized and highly disciplined. By nature you are persistent and able to stick to a task until it's done right. You enjoy stability and can tolerate routine more than most. Athough you seldom instigate change, you are a major player in seeing that when approved these changes become reality. If you're Active in assertiveness (above 50 percent), you are decisive in your decision making, but also cautious, usually going by the book. This keeps you out of trouble but is sometimes perceived by others as being inflexible. In attitude you are a team player but have difficulty in respecting anyone you feel is unorganized or detail-shy. Your leadership style can gravitate to a more authoritarian technique, retaining a lot of control as your group name suggests. If you are Receptive in assertiveness, the story on decision making, leadership, and relationships is a little different. In this case you have more difficulty in making decisions, especially if they involve directing others' behavior. In sales you sometimes need to remind yourself that the process of selling is more emotional than technical.

You are probably less interested at this point in pursuing a leadership role, preferring to keep a lower profile. In relationships you are loyal and a team player, but since you don't express your real feelings very often you can be manipulated by others whom you feel are not as competent as yourself. This can build resentment if unchecked over time. If you are a Control group Receptive it wouldn't hurt to be a little more opinionated and assertive, within reason.

Perhaps the greatest challenge to those in the Control category is to keep flexible to change and be tolerant of others less gifted. This is especially true if your Control rating is high and your Color rating is below 50 percent. Here you would be **Control Intense.** *However, if both your Control and Color scores are above 50 percent you are a Control Moderate. You would enjoy all the qualities of the Control group, but you would also avoid, to a greater degree, the downsides just discussed, being more accepting of change.*

Given the fact that you have the discipline part mastered, you have some excellent opportunities open to you. For instance, if you are **Control Intense,** it would probably be a great benefit to try to increase your Color profile by experiencing new things outside your normal comfort zone. It would also be helpful to occasionally try to instigate change; most Control Intense individuals can sometimes resent change, because they're usually the ones who have to do all the work implementing it for the team. Plus there is a period in any change cycle subject to confusion and error. This admittedly is distasteful to the Control Intense. However, if you can occasionally instigate the change yourself, it helps you to expand your vision and see the big picture rather than just the details. In sales, if you are Control Intense, even though your sales are efficiently executed, your volume may be low because of your passion for detail.

As a Control group individual you are in an excellent position to increase your performance by adding more color and variety to your game plan. This is especially true if you are Control Intense and, again, less of a concern to a Control Moderate. Remember, everything must change, and change can be your friend.

The Balanced Group ◈

If your Color versus Control scores *are within* 15 points of each other, you are in the Balanced group; and, obviously, the closer your scores are to each other, the more balanced you become.

If both your Color and Control scores are above the 50 percent mark, you are a **Balanced Moderate**. If at least one score is below 50 percent yet still within 15 points of the other score, you are a **Balanced Intense** individual. In addition, there are two minor descriptions for the Balanced group: Those who are Active, with an assertiveness rating above 50 percent, and those who are Receptive, with an assertiveness rating below 50 percent. Most of the information below applies to both of these groups; there are some differences, however, between Balanced Active and Balanced Receptive, which will be pointed out.

Being in the Balanced group, you're endowed with a good mix of both talent and discipline. This means you have the ability to produce new ideas and, most important, to make them into a reality. With your assertiveness rating above 50 percent, you also have the willingness and confidence to express your ideas to others. This makes you able to tackle the world of sales, which requires you to be adaptable while also attending to detail. In relationships you possess empathy toward others, but you also firmly stand up for what you believe in. You have the ability to be a team player, but you also like to lead. In your leadership style you often fall between the authoritarian and the democratic leader. This means you can discern how much freedom to give subordinates, but also when to exert more control. Of course, the lower your Color and Control rating, the less pronounced these qualities are. Please note that if you are at the outside limits of the Balanced group, that is, your Color and Control scores are 12 to 15 points apart, you may find it helpful to gain extra insight by also reading the description of the group you scored the highest in.

If you are a **Balanced Intense** with a Color or Control score below 50 percent, depending on your goals, you may want to find ways to enhance and raise your lower score to meet the challenge you're facing.

If your assertiveness rating is below 50 percent in the Receptive range, you are probably not as extroverted and may be more cautious and reserved when expressing your ideas and opinions to others. You are a good team player, able to relate well, but you probably prefer to keep a lower profile. This is true in the leadership role as well.

In looking at the overall Balanced category, perhaps the greatest challenge you face, especially if your totals are high, is to make sure you pick a big enough vision and goal to accommodate your abilities. To do this, you must constantly set new goals. Remember, nothing can limit you but you! Go for it!

INCREASING YOUR COLOR AND CONTROL RATING

Color

The key to making any change is to realize the benefit that change can bring. Like everything in life, there has to be a big why before there's a will. Consider the following benefits to adding more color to your life:

- Increased recognition for your abilities and accomplishments
- Better sociability and understanding of people
- Greater adaptability to change
- Less danger of burnout due to boredom and repetition
- Liberation from fears and self-imposed barriers, limiting your career potential

Here are some suggestions to enhance your Color capacity:

1. Enroll in a public speaking forum like Toastmasters or Dale Carnegie.

2. Take up an art form like painting, writing or a musical instrument — don't worry about being good, just indulge in the new experience.

3. Have your wardrobe evaluated and, if need be, upgrade with quality to reflect style, not fads.

4. Form a Brain Trust or Master Mind group. This will increase your circle of friends.

5. Change your reading material to include more biographies and self-help material.

6. Take up a new sport you've never seriously engaged in.

7. Become a Master Conversationalist. Learn to use humor and interesting stories to make your point.

8. Leave time each week for unplanned, spontaneous activity.

9. Develop a Trademark. Whether it's business cards, stationery, a nickname, or just an emphasis on quality, every major company has a slogan. What's yours? Whether it's subtle or bold, a trademark well done is colorful and can bring a measure of pride and recognition to you.

10. Get a Color Coach. This is someone strong in the area of Color who will volunteer to help you bolster this area. As payment, offer to be their Control Coach if that's your strength and their need.

Control

The greatest benefits to adding more control to your life are:

- The realization of your goals, as opposed to just dreaming about them.
- Sizable reduction in your anxiety level.
- The disappearance of procrastination and its harmful effects.
- More dependability, which will result in consideration for promotions and greater responsibility.
- Better customer service and long-term customer retention. Less needless errors and foul-ups.
- Increased performance and productivity, especially in sales.
- Better use of referrals and more add-on sales, resulting in bigger and more consistent income.

Here are some suggestions to increase your Control capacity:

1. Engage in time-Management and goal-setting seminars. Evaluate your strengths and weaknesses.

2. Only commit to that which you have sworn to deliver. Make your word mean something. This will help curtail extremes and impulsiveness.

3. Build a better relationship with your company's secretaries, administrative assistants, and support team. Find out their goals and make them aware of yours. Build a system of recognition and rewards for those who help you carry out your job.

4. Clean out your desk, office, and car of all unnecessary paper and clutter. Throw out most everything that isn't crucial and you haven't used in three months.

5. If you're self-employed or you don't have a support team, hire someone part or full time to handle your details. (Don't throw away dollars picking up pennies).

6. Take 15 to 30 minutes each day to handle mail and direct correspondence. Let nothing stay on your desk; respond immediately.

7. Utilize computers (and appropriate software) to organize business and personal information.

8. Don't take your major talent for granted. Spend time getting better and keeping informed with industry magazines and articles.

9. Study the most successful people in your field and duplicate their detailed work plans and systems.

10. Get yourself a Control Coach. This is someone who will volunteer to help monitor and raise your control skills. Be sure to make yourself totally accountable to them on a daily or weekly basis. They should have access to your records and appointment book. As payment, offer to act as their Color Coach, if they have the need.

Colorful

Controlled

1. Develop and practice a positive attitude.

   Be positive, but always choose reality-based action.

2. Be a fierce competitor with a killer instinct.

   Compete to achieve your own goals; elevate those you have defeated; beware of the pride trap.

3. Show emotion, especially your excitement.

   Discover what others are emotional about and shift your emotional excitement to fulfilling their needs.

4. Develop a strong personality with an identity of your own.

   Never overshadow others to the point where they feel neglected. Always be a team player. Serve someone.

5. Be a great communicator.

   Be a better listener.

6. Be flexible and tolerant of yourself and others.

   Don't compromise your integrity and values.

7. Learn to use and appreciate humor.

   Don't engage in humor that will hurt or offend others.

8. Keep your eye on the big picture. Don't major in the miniature.

   Make provisions to have the details and your paperwork attended to.

9. Be a willing teacher to the next generation.

   Be an open-minded student of the past and present generation.

The Plaid Counterbalance to Success

Colorful   **Controlled**

10. Develop a tough hide and become goal oriented. | Find a purpose that outlives your goals, and keep a tender heart.

11. Accept the challenge of leadership. | If the situation demands it, be a satisfied follower.

12. Expect greatness from yourself and others. | Never be shocked at the frailty of the human being.

13. Again, find a personal trademark. | Keep it appropriate and in good taste.

14. Be loyal. | Be loyal.

15. Become a student of your family history. | Develop your own traditions and heritage.

16. Read at least one book a month. | Turn off the TV. Turn on a book.

17. Learn to relax and have fun. | Always earn this right.

18. Stand tall and have faith in your abilities. | Get on your knees and pray for divine guidance and strength.

The Plaid Counterbalance to Success (*cont'd*)

RECOMMENDED READING

A reader today, a leader tomorrow.

Alexander, Scott. *Rhinoceros Success*. Self-published, 1980.
Chilton, David. *The Wealthy Barber*. Rocklin: Prima
  Publishing, 1991.
Forbes, B. C. *Thoughts on the Business of Life*. Tarrytown,
  N.Y.: Triumph Books, 1992.
Maxwell, John. *Be a People Person*. Wheaton, Ill.: Victor
  Books, 1989.
O'Brien, Michael. *Vince Lombardi*. New York: Quill, 1987.
Phillips, Donald T. *Lincoln on Leadership*. New York:
  Warner Books, 1992.
Swartz, David. *The Magic of Thinking Big*. New York:
  Prentice Hall, 1992.
Williams, Arthur Lynch, Jr. *All You Can Do Is All You Can
  Do*. Nashville, Tenn.: Oliver-Nelson, 1988.

Classics

Carnigie, Dale. *How to Win Friends and Influence People*.
  New York: Pocket, 1982.
Hill, Napoleon. *Think and Grow Rich*. New York: Fawcett,
  1960.
Hopkins, Tom. *How to Master the Art of Selling*. New York:
  Warner, 1980.
Living Bible, The. Wheaton, Ill.: Tyndale, 1971.
Ziglar, Zig. *See You at the Top*. New York: Ingram, 1977.

To contact Barry Munro's office, write or call:
Barry Graham Munro
P.O. Box 1664
Woodstock, GA 30188
(404) 924-0886

INDEX

Made in the USA
San Bernardino, CA
17 May 2020